Teaching Prayer in the Classroom

TEACHING PRAYER in the CLASSROOM

CLASSROOM

Experiences for Children and Youth

DELIA HALVERSON

A Griggs Educational Resource
Published By Abingdon Press
Nashville

TEACHING PRAYER IN THE CLASSROOM:
EXPERIENCES FOR CHILDREN AND YOUTH

Copyright © 1989 by Abingdon Press

This book is printed on acid-free paper.

ISBN 0-687-41100-9

Library of Congress Cataloging-in-Publication Data

Halverson, Delia Touchton.
   Teaching prayer in the classroom : experiences for children and
youth / by Delia T. Halverson.
      p.   cm.—(A Griggs educational resource)
   ISBN 0-687-41100-9 (alk. paper)
   1. Prayer—Study and teaching. 2. Christian education of
children. 3. Christian education of young people. I. Title.
BV214.H26   1989
248.3'2'07—dc20   89-6772
                                                                        CIP

Scripture quotations are from the Good News Bible unless otherwise noted -
Old Testament: Copyright © American Bible Society 1976:
New Testament: Copyright © American Bible Society 1966, 1971, 1976

Manufactured by the Parthenon Press at
Nashville, Tennessee, United States of America

CONTENTS

INTRODUCTION

Teachers in the church have the responsibility of creating an atmosphere in the classroom that enables students to grow in their relationship with God. Faith is a response to our relationship with God. Our beliefs may change and vary as we grow through life experiences. The relationship with God can begin at an early age and mature in a very personal way.

Much of the content of curriculum you use includes information about the Bible and beliefs that are compatible with your denomination. Unless the students learn how to apply what they learn to their lives every day and develop a relationship with God that is the heart of their faith, what they learn remains impersonal. All of the "knowledge" becomes as Paul's statement to the Corinthians, "If I speak in the tongues of men and of angels, but have not love, I am only a noisy gong or a clanging cymbal" (I Cor. 13:1, RSV). The personal relationship between the student and God becomes the artery for that love to develop, and prayer is the muscle of that artery.

Often, as I hold workshops and seminars for parents and teachers across the country, I am asked, "How can I help my children pray?" Many people feel they have an inadequate prayer life and are afraid to pray with children. Prayer is simply talking to God. Just as our conversations with a new friend become more comfortable as our friendship matures, our prayers (or conversations) with God will become more comfortable as we seek out those opportunities to speak to God and develop that friendship.

Students learn more frequently by our modeling than by our instructions. This book will help you find ways to model prayer and to guide the students in developing their own conversations with God.

A two-year-old friend of mine, Jana, helped me realize just how effective such modeling can be when she and her mother had lunch with me one day. We were on the deck of my house, sitting at a big patio table. Jana's mother asked her if she would like to say the blessing. I have always cautioned parents not to use prayer as a "show off" time. Jana's parents had moved away from our community before she was born and had recently returned. Since I had not known Jana personally for very long, I was not sure how she would react to the request. However, I should have had faith in the training of her parents. I was just unaware that such a comfortable feeling with prayer could be natural in such a young child.

Jana settled down in one of the large chairs and bowed her head. She began, "Dear God, thank you for the food. Thank you for the sandwich and for the apples and the milk. Lee is at a birthday party today, so she isn't with us. After we eat we are going to the party too, and I will swim in the pool. Daddy won't be there though, so he can't tease me. That's all. Amen."

Jana ministered to me. Her prayer contributed to my own growth in faith. Through the lives of children we grow, and our growth in turn models our faith to the children. We are in this faith journey together, sharing our God-relationship with each other.

DELIA T. HALVERSON

CHAPTER 1

WHAT IS PRAYER?

In years past, the primary prayers of the church were formal expressions, using eloquent words. Because our hymnals and books of prayer contain many such formal prayers, and because we often hear only polished prayers from the pulpit, many people assume that praying is something that they cannot do.

Prayers with eloquent words began as prayers from the heart, but when we repeat them often or if the words are not natural with us, we sometimes close our minds to the meanings of such prayers. Simple prayers from the heart are just as effective as, or maybe more effective than, a written prayer that has come down to us from our church heritage. I believe that every one of us has inwardly prayed a simple prayer at some time when we had a great need to communicate with God. It may have been something as simple as "God, give me strength!" These prayers are heard by God as personally as those from the pulpits of churches.

It has been suggested that memorized or traditional prayers are like practicing strokes on the edge of a pool. The practice is important, but until we let ourselves into the water and feel it uphold and support us, we cannot experience true swimming. Until we begin to wade out into the person/God relationship that we call prayer, we cannot experience true praying.

Praying is a conversation with God. Even a two-year-old such as my friend Jana, whom I mentioned in my introduction, can begin having simple conversations with God. If your students are older and still uncomfortable with prayer, there are methods in this book that will help to ease them into prayer opportunities.

A teacher who wants to help students grow in prayer must first be in prayer himself or herself. The teacher needs to pray in order to grow in personal relationship with God, and the teacher needs to pray for the students daily while working with them. Adapt the following prayer calendar to your class by dividing your students among the five weekdays. Use the calendar each day during your prayer time.

A Teacher's Prayer Calendar

Sunday	**Praise God!**	Thank God for all your students and allow your love for them to EXPLODE!
Monday	**Pray For:**	John who squirms. Sharon who seldom talks. Karen who talks constantly.
Tuesday	**Pray For:**	Jason who's torn between father and stepfather. Marv who keeps his hands dirty. Glenda who wants to answer every question.
Wednesday	**Pray For:**	Steve who is always late. Wade who needs more attention. Judy whose feelings are often hurt.
Thursday	**Pray For:**	Greg who is small for his age. Anne who always wants to please. Henry whose mother died last year.
Friday	**Pray For:**	Becky who is shy. Maria who smiles constantly. Chris who picks on Becky.
Saturday	**Pray For:**	Your church and your teaching ministry, and allow God to work through you. Share God's grace.

God, Our Personal Friend

Prayer develops a friendship with God. When you meet a new person that you would like to have as your friend, how do you go about developing that friendship? You do not pull out some sort of pre-written words that talk about friendship and relationships and stand before the person reciting the words. You try to find out all that you can about that person, and you reveal yourself to that person, so that you can find and appreciate the opinions and experiences that you have in common.

If God is to be our personal friend, then we must approach God as we would approach a new friendship. We must express our appreciation, we must share our everyday experiences, and we must be open in all that we do and all that we think.

But, you say, God knows all that there is to know. God knows that I appreciate the gifts of this earth. God knows that I have done wrong. Why must I thank God, or why must I confess what God already knows? A good friend is likely to understand that you appreciate his or her kind acts toward you, but when you express it verbally, a closer bond develops between you. Even if your friend knows you have wronged someone, and you know that the wrong does not threaten your friendship, there will be a strain on your relationship until you openly discuss the wrong-doing with your friend. The strain comes from your own holding back, from your own reservations.

Sometimes we can better understand prayer if we look at the different types or elements in our prayers. The remainder of this chapter will discuss prayers of adoration, confession, thanksgiving, supplication, and intercession.

The ACTS of Prayer

By using the word ACTS, we can remember four important elements in our prayer life. At the end of the chapter you will find suggestions for ways to help students learn these words and definitions.

A doration
C onfession
T hanksgiving
S upplication

From early biblical times, there was reference to the "fear of God." For biblical people, this phrase did not hold the same meaning that we connect with the word "fear" today. It was used when the writer was speaking of the "awe" of God.

However, *adoration* is even more than that. We can be in awe of the power of the split atom, but that awe does not cause us to worship it or to look to that power for strength and help. There must be a personal relationship in adoration. It is more like the simple term "looking and loving." We look to God, admiring what God has done for us and in awe of all of God's power, yet there is a personal loving that goes out from us in response to the personal love that we feel from God.

In *confession*, we meet God and accept the whole truth about ourselves. Confession is difficult without having experienced adoration. When we accept the love God gives us, and we experience our love for God that adoration brings, then we feel confident in opening ourselves and revealing our whole self to God. We will look at confession closer in the next chapter when we talk about ages of children.

One definition for sin is our separation from God. If an act separates us from God, then it is something that we need to confess in order to right our relationship with God. Often we get hung-up on particular "sins" when actually these are only symptoms of the real sin, the real thing that separates us from God. An example of this might be anger. Anger in itself is only a feeling, and neither right nor wrong. However, an attitude that we may have that causes anger, or the way that we express our anger, may be a sin. Perhaps our attitude is a determination to always have our own way; or perhaps we express our anger by hitting another person. These are the things that we need to look at in our confession to God.

We can help students look at why they got "mad" and their responsibility in venting their anger, instead of simply telling them that they musn't get mad. The blanket statement, "I'm sorry," can become trite if we don't dig deeper into what caused our feelings or why we reacted the way we did.

Thanksgiving is an easy type of prayer. Our beginning prayers as small children are usually prayers of thanksgiving. It is always easier to say thank you than to say "I was wrong," or to dig into our sins and say "I am sorry."

Prayers of thanksgiving can be spontaneous as well as planned prayers. Look for thanksgiving opportunities throughout the day. Help students consider all that they have to be thankful for, including disappointments and failures that help us grow. With the joy of thanksgiving, we can enter into a creative partnership with God.

Supplication is a word seldom used today. Petition is another word for this act of prayer. However, because our petitions of today usually apply pressure for change, we can often get the wrong idea about the petitions in a prayer. Pounding away at God does not make for a creative partnership. In the following story, two people come to God in prayer in two different ways.

> Bob was a member of a church we belonged to several years ago. He was actively involved in the church when he discovered that he had cancer. His wife attended and participated in programs. Their teenage daughters were in the youth group.
>
> As Bob's fight with cancer progressed, his wife sought spiritual help elsewhere. She found a church that gave her a special formula for prayer and told her that with that formula and deep faith, Bob would be healed.
>
> When physical healing did not take place, Bob's wife blamed it on his lack of faith and divorced him. Her church encouraged her to "rid herself of the stumbling block in her own faith."
>
> The teen daughters were forced to decide between their mother, who believed that she had found new spiritual understanding, and their father, who was dying of cancer but petitioned God for the help he needed to deal with his stressful situation, still holding onto the love that he knew God gives.
>
> The teenage girls had two types of petition prayers, or prayers of supplication, modeled for them. The mother petitioned God to heal so that she might have a physically whole husband. The father's petition gave him the ability to be in tune with God as a partner in his life. Even though the father was not healed physically, his petition released his body and mind so that he could establish a partnership with God. He received the inner healing that helped him through the final months of his life. [1]

The youth in this story experienced two different models and were forced to make choices and judgments that were difficult. We model Christian lifestyles in our prayers as well as in our living. What messages are we sending to them? There are times when it is important to help children and youth recognize that we are all working through our own faith journey and what is important in that journey for one may be different for another.

The prayer of supplication might be looked at as a sort of senior/junior partnership with God, in which the junior partner recognizes needs and the senior partner is aware of the needs and helps the junior partner to grow in achieving those needs. If the senior partner were to simply meet those needs without the junior partner's conscious efforts, then there would be no growth.

When we recognize our needs and petition God, we recognize that God is in control of the world and of our lives. We give our wants and desires over to God, instead of pleading with God to "come over to our side." Prayer is not a matter of playing sides and persuasion, but a matter of creative partnership. When we realize that God is in charge, our prayers of supplication will reflect this. Jesus modeled supplication for us when he prayed, "not my will, but thine be done." God will give us strength and insight to live our lives as effectively as possible.

Prayers of Intercession

Adoration automatically brings love for others, as we realize that we are created in relationship with others through the mind of God. First John 4:20 tells us that the acts of loving God and loving others are natural partners. This God-created relationship with others makes intercessory prayer natural.

Bishop Lance Webb, in his book *The Art of Personal Prayer*, describes intercessory prayer as loving another person, in God. It is a loving surrender of the other person to God—just "showing" God the person and your love for that person. It is not a magical force to get the person to "change," but a loving relinquishment of the other person, whether that person changes or not, and acknowledging to God that we relinquish the person with no strings attached. It's hard, because we do this for awhile, then we quite naturally pull the person back again.

True intercessory prayer lifts the burden off our shoulders and puts it in God's hands. If we try to "persuade" God by praying properly and for the correct amount of time, then we keep the burden on our shoulders. Intercessory prayer is like lending our minds and hearts out to God, but this requires a surrender of our will. When we pray in an act of giving-over rather than asking, we find release.

Even the skeptics look to "the power, whatever it is" when those that they love are in trouble. Praying for others seems to be universal and a part of the depth of our nature. Just as the forces of electricity were in the world from the beginning, and it took discovery of the source and of channels in order for us to use it, God created and set up channels or paths for us to love and care for each other. Intercessory prayers are the channels that we are discovering, making a connection between us and other people. Without intercessory prayer, our world is simply wound up to run. Prayer completes the circuit.

Bishop Webb suggests three steps in praying for others:

1) Wait in the presence.
2) Be willing to give yourself.
3) Give the one for whom you pray to God.[2]

In praying, even for those who persecute us (as Jesus taught in Matthew 5:44), we are also changed. We see the person for whom we are praying as God sees that person. The situation and relationship changes so that God can act. Prayer sets the stage and frees us to be open to God's guidance.

When we live our prayers, then our prayers and life are one. Sometimes we never know what effect our prayers have on the other person. In intercessory prayer, spiritual victory happens whether the physical and immediate outcome is what we expected or not. Physical healing without the spiritual healing is useless in our ministry for God.

"Why doesn't God answer my prayer?"

Most teachers have had a student ask this question. It is important that we stress that praying is not some magical formula that brings about just what we want. We need to help the students realize that prayer is conversation and our commitment to God, lining up our lives with God.

When we do ask God for specifics, sometimes the answer may be "no," but God never allows anything in our lives that we can't handle with God's help. We must realize that when the answer is no, then the "yes" part comes when God gives us the peace to live with the situation. Help students to think "Yes, I can make it through this, with God's help." In Phillipians 4:13 perhaps we should insert the word "Yes" in order to be more affirmative. "*Yes,* I have the strength to face all conditions by the power that Christ gives me."

Aids in Helping Children Identify Prayers

Younger children will take part in some of the elements of prayer, particularly in adoration and thanksgiving. Older preschool and younger elementary children can begin to deal with confession because it is personal. Most older elementary children and youth can grasp some understanding of prayers of supplication or petition. Simple prayers of intercession may be used at a variety of ages when we remember other persons in our prayers, such as asking God to be with the doctors who are helping a sick friend.

Although you may not want to introduce all of the "ACTS" elements of prayer or the term "intercessory prayer" until children are middle to late elementary age, there are many times when you can point out specific types of prayer as you use them.

Help younger children recognize prayers of adoration or thanksgiving by using the terms before or after you pray. This can be done by saying, "Let's pray a thanksgiving prayer for our food (friends, parents, flowers, etc.)." Or you might say, "When I see the tiny ants that God created I know we have a great God. Let's say a prayer that tells how we adore God."

Children who can understand telling someone "I'm sorry" can realize that confessing is telling God that you are sorry, and we can begin to name such prayers.

In chapter five I suggest that students learn to bring people who are special into their hearts in prayer. As you talk about such prayers with older children and youth, explain that sometimes we call these types of prayers intercessory prayers.

There are many methods you can use to help older students learn the types of prayers. The best way is to mention the type of prayer as you use the prayer. However, you do not want to confuse your students with "types" of prayers until they have had plenty of experience with being submersed in prayer. That would be like learning the alphabet before learning to speak. After you have worked with prayer in your classroom and the students feel comfortable in many prayer situations, use some of the methods below to help them learn to identify prayers.

Activities for learning types of prayers

1. Using some of the prayers of our heritage found in chapter three, help students identify the prayers or parts of prayers that are prayers of adoration, confession, thanksgiving, supplication, or intercession.

2. Create matching games by putting sentence prayers and types of prayers on individual cards. These can either be paired up or can be used for a concentration game. Here is an example:

God, the power of a waterfall amazes me.	Prayer of Adoration
I'm sorry that I hit Joe.	Prayer of Confession
Thank you, God, for the rain.	Prayer of Thanksgiving
God, I've studied, but help me with the test.	Prayer of Supplication
I want to help Jane, God. She's unhappy.	Prayer of Intercession

3. Place on a bulletin board the letters A, C, T, S, and I. Assign groups or individuals to write appropriate prayers for each letter: prayers of adoration for the letter "A," prayers of confession for "C," and so forth. Post the finished prayers. Use the prayers at appropriate times during the class—to open or close the session or as a litany during a worship time.

4. Initiate a prayer chain with older classes. When there is someone who needs prayer, begin the chain by calling one of the students and mention the type of prayer that is appropriate. That student calls another to pass on the message, and so on through the class.

Whatever methods you may use with your class, it is important to help the students feel at ease with prayer and not to apply pressure. Prayer is personal, and although we want our children to grow in their ability to share their prayers with others, we also want to keep it at a personal level.

1. Delia T. Halverson, *Helping Your Teen Develop Faith* (Valley Forge: Judson Press, 1985), pp. 50-51.
2. Lance Webb, *The Art of Personal Prayer* (Nashville: Abingdon, 1962), P.

CHAPTER 2

AGE LEVEL UNDERSTANDINGS OF PRAYER

C hildren and youth vary in their understandings of prayer and in their ability to express themselves to God. It is difficult to say, "You begin here with this age, and if your students are of that age, you begin there." However, there are certain concepts of prayer that young children cannot grasp, even when they feel free to express themselves. There are also some aspects of prayer that we need to consider with all students.

This does not mean that young children cannot worship and pray. In fact, many educators now believe that very young children are dealing with abstract thoughts, based on their limited experience.

I recall another two-year-old friend who visited me often in my office at the church. Katy was as comfortable talking to Rainbow, my goldfish, as she was playing in her room at home. One day, as she and her mother were leaving the church after preparing a classroom for Sunday, she told her mother, "I know what I want to be when I grow up. I want to be a god!"

Her mother asked, "Do you mean you want to be like Jesus and tell other people about God?"

"No," said Katy. "I want to be a god!"

Wisely, her mother asked, "Why do you want to be a god?"

Katy replied, "I want to be a god, because God loves everybody, and I want to love everybody."

At age two, Katy was dealing with some real theological concepts in the best way she knew how.

Each child deals with abstract thinking differently. In some classes there will be children who have a more developed abstract thought process than others. That thought process does not appear overnight, in full bloom, but comes on them slowly. As children gain more experience on which to base their thinking, and as their communication skills develop, they can relate to and communicate more abstract concepts.

Even as children begin to think abstractly, they have difficulty dealing with some of our theological concepts such as the Trinity, eternity, and salvation. They can repeat words that we may teach them in definition of these terms, but sometimes this is only lip service. They are working on their own experiences as they develop, and those experiences are limited.

When it is difficult for them to understand that their mother is also the daughter of their grandmother, we cannot expect them to understand our God as three persons. Since they cannot understand the finality of our earthly death, they have no way to relate a real understanding of what eternity means. Until they develop attitudes and values, they have no background for understanding salvation. Remember that young children are dealing with their own experiences.

Body Positions

We need not have specific body positions for prayer. When you are driving down a busy highway and feel a need to ask God for guidance, do you pull over to the side of the road and get down on your knees to pray? Praying is a living communication with God, and the sooner your students can realize that, the more at home they will feel in prayer.

There are two reasons for us to bow our heads and close our eyes in prayer: to block out the distractions around us and to humble ourselves. Young children cannot understand the abstract concept of being humble. And if you think requiring very young children to close their eyes during a prayer blocks out distractions, then you haven't watched a young child try to keep his or her eyes closed for a period of time. Keeping the eyes closed becomes a distraction in itself.

Open-eyed prayers are appropriate with young children. I have also used them with all ages, when we have had before us the very thing for which we were thanking God.

Prayers before snack time for young children can be an opportunity for an open-eyed prayer. Look at the snack, and ask the children to imagine what it tastes like as you pray. Then, as you continue to look at the snack, thank God for the food.

I recall a trip to a nearby park that we made with a second grade class. Spring was in its full color, and everywhere the flowers and shrubs seemed to shout praise to God. We used Psalm 96: 11-13:

> Be glad, earth and sky! Roar, sea, and every creature in you; be glad, fields, and
> everything in you! The trees in the woods will shout for joy when the Lord comes
> to rule the earth. He will rule peoples of the world with justice and fairness.

After talking about what we saw before us and how God made the whole world and all that was in it, we each stood in different directions, looking at some specific thing that was beautiful to us, and thanked God in our own minds.

Special Wording

Children and youth need no special wording in their prayers. We want this to be a natural relationship with God, so we want to use familiar words with them. Consider the word "bless." Many adults do not understand the meaning of the word, although we use it often. I can recall thinking as a child that I must be sure to "bless" everyone in my prayers each night, and if I happened to forget one person I was afraid that some terrible problem would befall that person. This was a hard burden for a seven year old to carry, as if I had the responsibility of the fate of those people on my shoulders.

"Bless" is not a magical word that keeps the person from evil. Although bless and intercession are not interchangeable, bless is loving another person in God. The prayer of intercession releases that person and sets up a channel for God to work.

With young children, perhaps it is more appropriate to express our thanks to God for these people as we pray instead of using the term "bless." Older elementary children and youth can begin to deal with the concept of blessing another person.

"Confess" is another word that children seldom use. In our society, a confession is usually reserved for a major crime. Simply saying "I'm sorry" to God may be more appropriate for children.

In formal prayers, the terms "thee, thou, and thine" are often used. These words are not used in our everyday language, and we may not fully understand them. They are a hold-over from the King James Version and lend a gentle sound to the prayer. However, we must remember that a prayer is not said for the way it sounds, but rather for the communication between the person praying and God. At the time of the writing of the King James Version, there were two sets of pronouns. The words "you and yours" were formal words, used only for royalty or superiors. The pronouns "thee, thou, and thine" were used for persons very close to you, such as your family. Therefore, referring to God as a "father" and using "thee, thou, and thine" placed the relationship with God on a very personal level. Over the years we have completely reversed the use of these words.

It is natural for adults to speak of God as our father or our parent. However, we need to be aware that some of our students do not have a positive father image in the home and some do not have a father at all. A child once told the teacher, "My father is mean to me. I can't pray to God as a father, but my mother is kind." The positive concept of God as a parent who is loving and kind is what we want to develop. Consequently, we need to be inclusive in our language about God so that God can be experienced in the loving way that Jesus intended when he said, "Our Father."

When our son was two, we had pancakes one morning. His father said, "These are delicious!" Sammie immediately argued with him that they weren't delicious, but they were pancakes. Young children sometimes have difficulty putting two definitions to a word. There are many ways to address God in a prayer. When we sometimes pray to God and sometimes pray to Jesus, we may give young children mixed signals. The concept of the Trinity is very abstract. Adults understand that Jesus was God in an earthly form, and occasionally we feel more at home praying to Jesus. However, we do not need to use such abstract ideas with young children. They have a lifetime to wrestle and come to grips with abstract theological concepts. It is better to use the term God in our prayers with young children, and help them appreciate Jesus as the person who taught us what God is like. As they grow older, they will better grasp the relationship of the Trinity that we hold so important. As the child's understanding of Jesus grows, it will become natural to pray sometimes to Jesus and sometimes to God.

Formal Prayers

The style of prayer will vary, depending on the content of your prayer and the age of your students. Older elementary children and youth can study some of the special prayers of the church. At this time you can begin talking about the different parts of such prayers and experiment with developing prayers that contain these parts. The ACTS of prayer that was discussed in the previous chapter is a good way to look at formal prayers.

Elementary children can begin wording prayers in a more formal way. These might be used in the congregational worship from time to time and printed in the bulletin. This gives the children an appreciation of their participation in the worship experience.

As some of us were growing up, we learned the words of the Lord's Prayer in the school classroom. Since this is no longer possible in public school, it is important that we help children learn the prayer in the church school. I realize that young children cannot understand many of the words. However, once a child takes part in congregational worship, I think it is important for him or her to begin to learn the words. It will help the child to feel a part of the total church family by praying the prayer along with the rest of the congregation. Youth may also need help with the meaning. Chapter three will cover the Lord's Prayer in more detail.

The guidelines below will give you help as you work with your students in prayer. The following chapters will give you concrete suggestions for ways to move them into a personal relationship with God through prayer.

NURSERY

Associate prayer with good things.

Pray prayers of thanksgiving and praise.

Pray with the child as if you are talking to God. Begin the relationship with God.

Use simple language: "you" and "your," not "thee," "thou," and "thine."

No particular body position is necessary.

Child need not always close eyes.

Giving thanks for food after eating makes more sense to this age child.

KINDERGARTEN

Provide some opportunities for prayer.

Pray spontaneous prayers. "Talk" to God.

Prayer can be two to five short sentences of everyday speech. Pray what the child understands.

Religion is private; prayer is not a time to show off. Be cautious of asking child to pray before guests.

Evening prayers: Talk over happy times of the day, kindnesses, how God helped—then pray. Begin requests for help: "Help me to remember to cross the street carefully . . . to take turns . . . to help others." Older kindergartners may pray for someone else: "Help the doctor to help Johnny."

Begin to distinguish between asking Daddy for toys and asking God to help us take turns. God works through people for physical needs.

GRADES 1-3

Continue praise and thanksgiving.

Let the child compose his or her own prayers.

Create litany prayers together.

Give opportunities for sentence prayers after discussion of what we are thankful for—don't force the child to pray.

Acknowledge need for forgiveness.

Encourage prayers asking for help, making them more specific than before.

GRADES 4-6

Encourage personal and private worship. Provide devotional material.

Help child to appreciate prayers in formal worship.

Study prayers in hymnal for special occasions.

Continue prayer as close relationship with God.

Encourage growth so that this relationship with God is there when child is more independent. [1]

GRADES 4-6

Continue to encourage personal and private worship.

Expand use of formal prayers and learn about the authors.

Include intercessory prayers in your class plans.

Prayers for guidance will help youth over difficult time.

YOUTH

Continue to encourage personal and private worship.

Expand use of formal prayers and learn about the authors.

Include intercessory prayers in your class plans.

Prayers for guidance will help youth over difficult time.

1. Delia T. Halverson, *Helping Your Child Discover Faith* (Valley Forge, Pa.: Judson Press, 1982), pp. 118-19.

CHAPTER 3

MEMORIZED PRAYERS

We often hear amusing stories of childrens' interpretations of memorized prayers. Dr. Millie Goodson was professor of Christian education at Scarritt Graduate School when I heard her tell about her niece's version of the Lord's Prayer. She began, "Our Father, who aren't in heaven, how do you know my name?"

An adult may consider such an incident cute or amusing. But if we look more closely at this child's interpretation, we see that she was reaching out to God, with a need that God be personal enough to know her name. Even memorized prayers need to be personal, because prayer is a very personal communication between individuals and God.

Left Brain/Right Brain

In Matthew 22:37 Jesus gave the Pharisee the greatest commandment, "Love the Lord your God with all your heart, with all your soul, and with all your mind." Jesus recognized the importance of using all of our mind, and I believe this is necessary in our prayer life as well as in our study.

In recent years I have read much about the functions of the left and right sides of our brains. Scientists believe that the left side of our brain is used for rational and analytic thinking. This is the side that memorizes well. The symbolic, intuitive, meditative, and visual facets of our prayer life are handled by the right side of our brain. In order to have a healthy prayer life, it is important that we learn to function with both sides of our brain.

Some of us function better with one side or the other. Memorization comes quite easy for some of us while it is very hard for others. It is important that no student feel that he or she is inadequate because memorization is difficult.

I recently spoke with a teacher who was using rewards for memorization. I shared with her the fact that I have never been able to memorize. I didn't learn the alphabet until I was in the third grade, and I have memorized the books of the Bible three times, and cannot recite them to you today. When I was a child, other students were able to memorize easily while I would practice and practice, only to reverse a phrase or substitute a synonym. This Sunday school teacher responded in surprise, "Why, I have always had such ease with memorization that I thought when a student didn't memorize something it was only because of lack of study." Many teachers assume everyone likes to memorize. Memorization comes from repeated use of something, or when something becomes memorable. Memorization for memorization's sake is often not lasting, and motivation for such is hard to come by for most students.

You will also find that some of your students memorize easily but have difficulty verbalizing their thoughts in prayer. This may be particularly true with older students who have never prayed in public. By using suggestions in the next two chapters, you can help these students to feel more confident.

Your class sessions need to have a balance of both types of prayer. Be aware of your students and their needs. Since prayer is a personal and private experience—even when shared aloud, be understanding with the students.

Whether you are using memorized or spontaneous prayer, let me suggest that students always be given the option of public participation in prayer. I would discourage the practice of "going around the circle" in prayer, but rather begin a prayer time yourself and close it with a memorized prayer that everyone knows or is learning, suggesting that anyone feel free to offer a prayer in between.

Memorization Aids

In order to pray a memorized prayer, it is important for the student to understand the words. Be aware of the ages of your students, and do not select prayers with abstract meanings for children who still think concretely. Go through the prayer, word by word, and explain any unfamiliar words in simple language. If you are using a prayer from our Christian heritage that uses "thee" or "thou," explain that these are ways of saying "you" that were used a long time ago. Older children and youth may be interested in the information in chapter two that relates to these terms.

Students who read can work on understanding the meaning of words in a memorized prayer with a card game. Write all of the words or phrases of the prayer on cards. On the back of any card with a word or phrase that is unfamiliar, write the definition in a different color. Using a copy of the prayer, the student will arrange word/phrase cards in order. Any words that are new or unfamiliar may then be turned over to display the definition. The prayer may be read using the definition cards first. Then the student turns the definition cards back over and practices the prayer.

It is a great help for students to see the words as they memorize the prayer. I like to use a pocket board with memorization. A pocket board is made by taking a poster board and creating long pockets across the board with folded strips of long paper:

Here are directions for making a Pocket Chart:
Supplies:
- 1 piece of poster board or heavy cardboard (22" x 28")
- 2 three inch strips of paper (may use freezer or shelf paper), each 30 inches long.

- Transparent tape
- Index cards (same number as there are words or phrases).

Procedure:

Fold the long strips of paper in half lenghwise. Placing the fold at the top, space evenly down the poster board (see illustration), taping them across the bottom and folding the ends around the edges of the poster board, taping them to secure.

Write words or phrases of the prayer at the top of 3 x 5 cards, and place them in order in the pockets. Read the prayer as a class several times, using all of the cards. Then each time you read the prayer, randomly remove one of the cards. Soon the class will be saying the prayer without the cards.

If your group is small, you can create the same learning experience by simply placing the cards, face up, on the floor or table and removing cards as you learn the prayer.

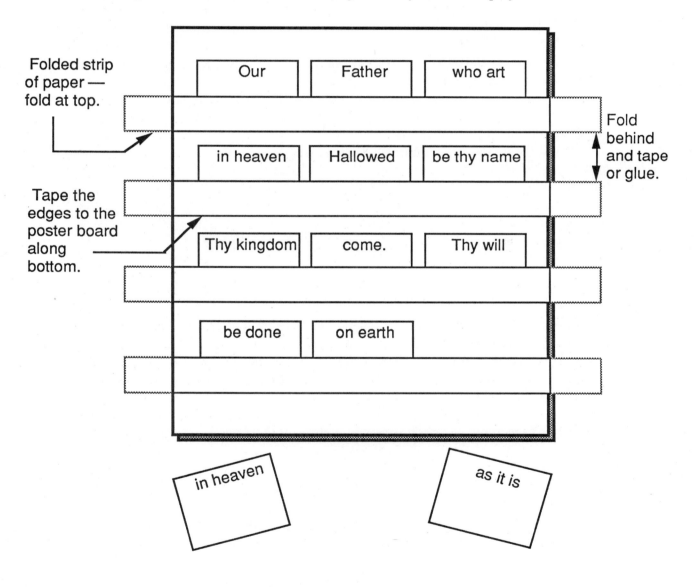

Psalm Prayers

The Book of Psalms is actually a book of songs and prayers. There are verses from many psalms that are appropriate for young children to learn, and whole sections that older children and youth can learn. The psalms were composed by different people over a long period of time and came to be a part of the Hebrew life and later an important part of the early church.

Some of the prayers in the psalms portray the personal feelings of an individual, and others are prayers that express the feelings of a group. There are prayers of praise and thanksgiving, and prayers for God's blessing. There are also prayers for help, forgiveness, protection, and salvation.

Many of the psalms are quoted in the New Testament, and Jesus frequently used psalms. From the early beginnings, they have always been a part of the Christian church, and we often use them in our worship today.

Be aware of different translations of psalms as you consider memorized prayers. If it is a psalm that is frequently used in worship, you may want to learn the version that is used by your church. Many of us learned passages of the psalms from the King James Version of the Bible, sprinkled with thees and thous. As suggested in the previous chapter, these words do not feel as natural to our children as they do to us. Since we want to help children feel at ease in talking with God, you might want to consider other translations. The Good News Bible presents Psalms in a very personal way. Youth will enjoy and benefit from using a variety of translations and paraphrases to compare use of language.

Because the ancient Hebrew poetry did not have rhyme and meter as we know it today, most of the translations are in the form of free verse. However, there is a parallelism that most translations have preserved. A statement is made at the beginning of the psalm, then repeated, sometimes in the exact words and sometimes in a modified fashion, throughout the psalm.

Below I have suggested several ways to involve your students in the psalms. The activity suggestions in the remaining chapters can also be adapted easily to psalms.

Activities Using Psalms

1) Students can pray psalms in a more personal way by substituting their own name at places where a personal pronoun is used.

2) Read the psalm in various translations and ask the students to point out how they vary in wording. Then ask them which words make the psalm more meaningful to us today and why.

3) Have the class help you create a litany, using passages of praise from psalms as the group response.

4) Using the suggestions under poetry prayers in chapter five, help the students create their own prayer psalms.

The following are examples of some appropriate Psalm passages for children. These may be read as their own prayers or memorized.

Psalm 8:1*a*	Psalm 30:12*b*	Psalm 104:1*a*
Psalm 9:1	Psalm 41:13	Psalm 118:28*a*
Psalm 9:2	Psalm 75:1*a*	

Psalm Prayers for Older Children

Psalm 5:1-3	Psalm 38:21-22	Psalm 63:1-5
Psalm 8 (all or part)	Psalm 51:1-2	Psalm 86:8-10
Psalm 9:1-2	Psalm 51:10	Psalm 90:1-2
Psalm 16:11	Psalm 51:15	Psalm 108:3-5
Psalm 19:14	Psalm 57:9-10	Psalm 119:89-91
Psalm 36:5-7	Psalm 61:1-3	Psalm 139:1-4

If you are teaching youth, consider using *Teaching and Praying the Psalms* by Donald Griggs to involve your students with the Psalms.

The Lord's Prayer

Children are primarily experiential and affiliative in their faith development. Therefore, it is of prime importance for them to feel a part of worship services and group experiences in the church.

The Lord's Prayer has words that make it primarily an adult prayer. However, because it is the central prayer that Christians everywhere use, I believe that it is important for children to begin to learn it as soon as they are a part of a congregation or other group using the prayer. Many of the words may be beyond their understanding, but the opportunity to "belong" far outweighs the problems of not grasping the words.

Young children need to know that this is a prayer that Jesus taught us to pray and one that Christians use everywhere. Words can be explained in simple terms, using some of the ideas listed below for elementary children. The wording of the prayer used here is from the Revised Standard Version of the Bible.

Our Father,   Because God is like a good father,
                                   Jesus used the word Father.
                                   By using the word "our" we realize
                                   that God loves all of us and wants us
                                   to work together.

who art in heaven,   The word "art" is an old way of saying
                                   "is." When we speak of God being in
                                   heaven, it does not mean far away, but
                                   rather that God is everywhere and
                                   greater than we can understand.

Hallowed be thy name.	"Hallowed" is a way of praising God, another word for holy, awe, or wonder.

Thy kingdom come,
   Thy will be done,
      On earth as
      it is in heaven.
	With these words we pray that all of us on earth will live as God wants, loving each other.

Give us this day **our daily bread;**	When we pray for "our daily bread," we realize that God made the world that produces food for us to eat. Food is also a part of God's plan, and God is a dependable God. We also realize that all of our daily needs are important to God. Notice that Jesus did not use *my* daily bread, but *our*. The prayer doesn't ask for everything we want each day, but for what we need.
And forgive us our debts,	We recognize that we all sin. The word "debt" is a very old word for sin. Sometimes when we pray the prayer we use the word "trespass," which in this context is another word for sin. The real meaning for sin is that we "separate ourselves from God." When we sin, we do something or think something that keeps us from being close to God. We ask God to forgive us, knowing that we are forgiven if we are truly sorry.
As we forgive our debtors	We also tell God that we forgive others of sins against us. We realize that we must forgive in order to set ourselves right with God.
And lead us not into **temptation.** **But deliver us** **from evil.**	A temptation is when we want to do something other than what God wants us to do. We realize that God's help is available for us and know that we will need it to follow God's good plan for us.

In most versions of the Bible, this is where Matthew's direct quotation from Jesus ends. However, as early as the end of the third century people were using this prayer in their worship services, and they found such joy over the words of the prayer that they just continued the prayer, using some of the words from 1 Chronicles 29: 10-13. The following words have been added by tradition and are commonly used with the passage from Matthew.

For Thine is the kingdom,	The close of the prayer again says
and the power,	that we believe that God is over all
and the glory,	the world and universe (kingdom) and
	is the greatest.
Forever!	We know that God is forever, with no end.
AMEN.	The word "amen" means "I agree,"
	or "May it be so."

Older children and youth can read the prayer. When you study the prayer in your classroom, bring in several translations of the Bible for the students to read. Remind them that the New Testament was first written in Greek, and that we have different versions because some Greek words do not have exact words that mean the same thing in English.

Explain that the wording that we pray in The Lord's Prayer has come about over the years, although we find the original form in Matthew 6:9-13. Luke carries a shorter version of the prayer in verses 2-4 of chapter 11.

We call this The Lord's Prayer because Jesus taught it to his disciples, and we often call Jesus Lord. Through the years the addition was used in the prayer, and it has been translated into many different languages. We now use it all over the world. Sometimes the wording may vary a little. For example, in English, some churches use the word "debts" and some use "trespasses." When it is translated into other languages there may be no exact word for some original word and the closest word will have to be used. But we are still praying it together, as Christians all over the world.

Historic Prayers

In our early church heritage, and through the years, many people have formed meaningful prayers, and we use some of them today when we pray together. Older children and youth can grasp the time element in history. It is important for them to have exposure to some of the prayers of our Christian heritage. Preface memorization of these prayers by using an experiential learning process, such as drawing illustrations of the prayer.

Using your church hymnal or other worship sources, locate prayers that you use regularly in your services. These prayers may be used as calls to worship, prayers of confession, offering prayers, and benedictions. Learning these prayers will help students to participate in worship. Look at the prayers that are used in your communion service. Discuss the word meanings and pray the prayer together often enough to become familiar with it so that they can participate naturally in the service. Many of these prayers use "thee" and "thou," and you will need to be aware that in church school classes we have sporadic attendance and a student may not have been in class when you explained the words before.

Art is an excellent way of introducing these historic prayers. By illustrating the prayers, you look at the meaning of the words and life situations relating to the prayer. Help your students appreciate the prayers that are used in your worship services through art. You may want to consider banners or posters that can be used in the sanctuary for a period after the classroom experience.

Heritage Prayers

Thou hast made us for Thyself, and our heart is restless, until they find rest in Thee.

St. Augustine, 354-450

Christ, be with me, Christ before me, Christ behind me,
Christ in me, Christ beneath me, Christ above me,
Christ on my right, Christ on my left,
Christ where I lie, Christ where I sit, Christ where I arise,
Christ in the heart of every one who thinks of me,
Christ in the mouth of every one who speaks to me,
Christ in every eye that sees me,
Christ in every ear that hears me.
Salvation is of the Lord,
Salvation is of the Lord,
Salvation is of the Christ,
May your salvation, O Lord, be ever with us.

St. Patrick, 389-461

May the road rise to meet you.
May the wind be always at your back
May the sun shine warm upon your face.
May the rains fall softly upon your fields
until we meet again.
May God hold you in the hollow of his hand.

Old Gaelic blessing

O Lord our God, grant us grace to desire thee with our whole heart, that so desiring, we may seek and find thee; and so finding thee we may love thee; and loving thee we may hate those sins from which thou hast redeemed us; for the sake of Jesus Christ.

St. Anselm, 1033-1109

Lord, make me according to thy heart.

Brother Lawrence, 1611-91

God be in my head, and in my understanding;
God be in my eyes, and in my looking;
God be in my mouth, and in my speaking;
God be in my heart, and in my thinking;
God be at my end, and at my departing.

Old Sarum Primer

Thou art never weary, O Lord, of doing us good. Let us never be weary of doing thee service. But, as thou hast pleasure in the prosperity of thy servants, so let us take pleasure in the service of our Lord, and abound in thy work, and in thy love and praise evermore. O fill up all that is wanting, reform whatever is amiss in us, perfect the thing that concerneth us. Let the witness of thy pardoning love ever abide in all our hearts.

John Wesley, 1703-91

Drop thy still dews of quietness,
Till all our strivings cease;
Take from our souls the strain and stress,
And let our ordered lives confess
The beauty of thy peace.

J.G. Whittier, 1807-92

CHAPTER 4

SPONTANEOUS PRAYER

It was Sunday morning, and the teacher and preschoolers were on their hands and knees, centering their attention on the floor. Before them marched a parade of ants, carefully moving crumbs of an abandoned cookie from the table to their home, somewhere outside. The teacher was saying, "Look at those tiny legs. God made the tiny ants and made them with such strength that they can carry crumbs bigger than they are. I thank you, God, for the chance to see your ants today."[1]

To persons passing in the hall, the scene may have appeared strange. But to the teacher and children, this was an experience in spontaneous prayer. Experiential opportunities are important for children's faith journey. Spontaneous prayer brings God out of the "there and then" and into the "here and now," helping children relate God to their own lives.

Spontaneous prayers are appropriate for all of us, whether we are young children or adults. We do not need to wait for a formal prayer time to thank God for a beautiful sunset or for an act of kindness from a friend. Whether you teach children or youth, there are times when spontaneous prayer can be a natural part of our living and learning together.

Talking-prayers work best in spontaneous situations. There's no need for some formal type of prayer, just simply talk with God. Depending on the situation, you may sometimes choose to keep your eyes open, smiling into the faces of the children or looking at the object about which you are praying.

Begin spontaneous prayer by talking about what you see or what you experience. As you work with prayer in the classroom, you will become alert to opportunities to pray spontaneously. You will also learn to weave such occasions into your curriculum. What follows are examples of ways to incorporate spontaneous prayer into the life you and your students share in the classroom.

As Children Arrive

As the children arrive, greet each one individually. By using their names, you let them know that you think they are important. Talk about how you thank God that he or she came today; that you are thankful that it is Sunday, and that you can all be together in the class. If you experienced something beautiful on the way to church, you might tell a child about it and say that you thank God for it. As your class feels more comfortable with spontaneous prayer, encourage the children to share their own experiences as they enter the classroom.

During Work Times

Activities during a class time need to be a part of the whole learning process. Most curriculum writers suggest activities that give experiences related to the purpose of the session. Be conscious of how your activities give the students experiences in faith, and look for opportunities to pray spontaneously about those experiences. If you prepare gifts for other people, thank God for the opportunity to share love with others. If you make some object that visually expands the purpose of the session, comment on the student's work and thank God for it. For younger children, acknowledge how much more capable they are of such work (cutting, pasting, drawing) than they were some months ago. Thank God for this growth.

Preschoolers' Play Times

As the preschoolers play, move around the room, listening to the activity among the students. In the housekeeping center, talk about families and how God planned for us to live together in families. Be sure to include all types of families: two parent families, one parent families, families with several generations, step-families, foster families, extended families. Thank God for families.

If the children are "preparing" a meal, talk about how God provides the food and how God's helpers care for it and get it from the farms to our stores for us to buy. Talk about how the children are "preparing" the meal just as their parents take care of them at home. Thank God for those who help by giving us food.

In the building or puzzle and book center, be alert to each child's developmental process. When a child is able to build a higher tower of blocks, or read new words, or piece a puzzle that was frustrating on a previous day, talk about how he or she is growing, just the way God planned. Thank God for this new growth. This can be done with a simple statement, "I thank God for the way you are learning to stack the blocks."

In Nature

Although most class sessions are usually held indoors, you can still find opportunities to share God's creation with the students and experience spontaneous prayer. Be aware of what is happening in nature, and talk about it, including prayers of thanksgiving in your conversation. Using suggestions from other chapters in this book, help the students create prayers about God's creation. Of course, you will need to be aware of the scientific understanding of the students you are teaching. Young children can understand simple thank you prayers for items in God's creation. Older children and youth can begin to grasp the miracles of the workings of God in the world.

On the morning following a rain, thank God for providing water for us and all living things. Then talk about the importance of water. After experiencing an electrical storm, older children can thank God for giving us electricity. The class might think of all the things that we would not have if God had not made electricity, or if persons before us had not used the brains that God gave them to learn how to use electricity.

As seasons change, talk with the students about the dependability of God that is shown in the seasons. Day following night, sprouting bulbs, the movement of the stars, and the tides are also signs of the dependability of God. Offer a thank-you prayer for such a dependable God. I've found youth and adults more appreciative of God's seasons when we speak openly of them.

Develop a nature table and ask students to bring items from God's creation for which we are thankful. This is appropriate not only for preschoolers who love show-and-tell, but also for elementary students. You may plan to have an encyclopedia or science reference book available at the table for the students to do a little research. As you have a worship or conversation time, encourage children to talk about what they brought for the table. After those who brought something and those who have researched it have shared, you can offer a prayer of thanks for everything, or you may create a litany using the suggestions from chapter six.

As You Eat Together

There may be occasions when your class will have a meal together. Often preschoolers will have a snack time during their classes.

Singing or memorized prayers are appropriate at snack times. Consider some of the suggestions in chapter three. Be conscious that some parents may have strict rules about singing at the table. Tell the children that singing a prayer is different from regular singing at the table. Help them understand that singing prayers is a way of praising God.

Vary your prayer experience at snack time. Sometimes you may want to thank God before you eat, and sometimes it is good to thank God after you have eaten, remembering how good it tasted. Try varying the prayer throughout the year. If you teach very young children and you plan to pray before eating, it may be wise to leave the snacks visible but not hand them out individually until after the prayer.

Planning Projects

Service projects may be as simple as making a thank you card for a custodian or a get well card for a classmate, or as involved as planning a parent/child project where you help to clean up or paint up an old person's home in the neighborhood. Elementary children and youth can think of their projects as ministry and see themselves as an outreach of the church.

All students can see such experiences as a way of sharing what they have learned with others. They can also understand that doing things for others, caring for them, showing them love, is done because Jesus taught us to live this way. This is a way of showing we love Jesus.

As you plan service projects with your class, take time to ask for God's guidance before you make a decision of what you will do. This may vary, depending on the age of your students. With younger students, a simple prayer will be appropriate, such as, "God, we want to help

_____. We ask you to be with us as we make plans to help. Amen."

With older students, you may want to lengthen the prayer to summarize the different choices that you have before you, then ask for guidance. After the decision has been made, ask God to be with you as you begin your ministry with whomever you are working.

Thanksgiving Prayers

Prayers of thanksgiving are appropriate for all ages and at any time of the year. When you include them in your daily life, they become "thanksliving" prayers. Be alert to the times in your curriculum when you can naturally include a prayer of thanksgiving. There will be sessions when you consider the workers of the church or other helpers in the community or at home, times when you consider mission projects that the church does, or times when you thank God for those in our past heritage who have contributed to our church.

Often in your curriculum, you will have suggestions for celebration. These times may come at the end of the session, or they may be woven into the session. Whenever it seems appropriate, take a moment for prayer. Sometimes a simple "Thank you, God, for such good times together," expresses the feelings of the group.

Don't forget times when you talk about the student's own gifts from God, their talents and abilities. Help them to see that God's gifts are not limited to musical or artistic talents. Assure them that an ability to listen to someone else's problem and let the person know that you care is a gift or talent from God. Offer thanks for these gifts.

Personal Relationships

Be aware of the relationships between your students. Young children often have difficulty sharing toys and need help in learning this art. Older children also have difficulties with relationships. For youth, relationships are a primary focus and concern. When relationships have been restored, you may want to pray a simple prayer of thanks with the students involved. This needs to be private and between the persons involved, not brought before the whole class.

Older preschool and elementary children can begin to use prayers of confession. It may be appropriate to suggest that the students think a silent prayer, telling God that they are sorry for whatever caused their broken relationship, then you may close with a sentence, thanking God for the healed relationship. The verse in 1 Peter 3:8a, "Finally, all of you, live in harmony with one another," (N.I.V.) may be appropriate here. Share the verse by simply stating that you are happy that they are learning to live together happily as it tells us to do in the Bible, then say the verse.

Developing Spontaneous Prayers

Periodically, tell students that you thank God that they came today or that you were able to all be together today. This may be done individually, not as a ritual, as they pass through the door, but spontaneously in conversations with the students. Help prayers to develop in a spontaneous way, taking prayer out of a routine context. In this way, they learn to turn to God any time and in all circumstances, instead of just at mealtimes or bedtimes.

Your spontaneous prayers in the classroom model this. As they become at ease with your praying naturally, they will begin to see opportunities to do so themselves. These personal prayers may come about through their inner thoughts, and you may never hear such spontaneous prayers spoken out loud. But be aware that you are laying the groundwork for that personal relationship between God and the student.

1. As told by Dr. Millie Goodson, Associate Professor of Christian Education, Scarritt Graduate School, Nashville, Tennessee.

CHAPTER 5

CREATING PERSONAL PRAYERS

Prayer is always personal, even when shared with other people. This chapter deals primarily with internal prayer, with personal conversation with God that need not be shared with others.

All children have worship experiences, even before they are old enough to verbalize what's going on inside. In fact, the lack of ability to verbalize may be one reason we often believe children are not able to worship at a young age.

One day as I stood in a party store, a two-year-old boy hung onto his mother, whining, as she tried to talk to the clerk. In an effort to keep the child quiet, the clerk tied a helium balloon on the young boy's wrist. The clerk was unaware, however, that she helped to create a worship experience for that child. As I watched the boy slowly pull the balloon down and watch it rise again into the air, I saw an expression of awe or worship for the power that controlled the balloon, a power greater than his.

We can lay the foundation for personal prayer with very young children, even before they can understand the words. As nursery workers hold and rock or play with babies, speaking prayers of thanks and love for the child begins to set the tone for the child's reaction to prayer.

For preschoolers, personal prayers are sometimes verbalized, even when no one else is around. Watch a three-year-old alone at play. Talking to him/herself, the child seems to carry on a conversation. Verbalization often helps the young child's thought process. Because of this, verbal direction or encouraging and enabling prayer may be particularly helpful for young children.

As you introduce personal prayer to older children and youth, talk about how Jesus taught us to pray by his example. Look at examples of Jesus' prayer life. Divide the students into pairs. Have each pair look up and read *one* passage.

Matthew 6:9*b*-13	Mark 1:35	Luke 5:15-16	John 11:41*b*-42
Matthew 14:18-21	Mark 14:36	Luke 6:12-16	John 12:27-28
Matthew 14:22-23	Mark 15:34	Luke 9:28-29	John 17
Matthew 19:13-14		Luke 10:21*b*-22	John 21:13
Matthew 26:26-29		Luke 23:34	
Matthew 26:36-43		Luke 23:46	
		Luke 24:30	
		Luke 24:50-51	

As the students look up the passages and recall the stories of Jesus' life, ask them to answer these questions. Tell them that they will need to read some of the verses before and after the reference in order to answer some questions.

When did Jesus pray? What was happening?

Where was Jesus when he prayed?

Who was with Jesus when he prayed?

What kind of prayer did Jesus pray?

Why do you think Jesus felt the need to pray?

Have each pair share their passage and their answers to the questions. Have the class discuss the last question together and how this relates to our need to pray. What do we learn about prayer from these examples of Jesus?

Silent or Meditative Prayer

Silent or meditative prayer may be new to your students. Usually, when we suggest silent prayer, we simply ask the students to close their eyes and pray to themselves. We may give them a suggestion of a subject for their prayers, but we seldom direct them as they immerse themselves in prayer. Just as memorized prayer is like practicing swimming strokes on the edge of the pool, a quiet inner communication with God can be compared to letting yourself go and feeling the cool water support and refresh you on a hot summer day.

Marlene Halpin has done extensive work with children and prayer. In her book *Puddles of Knowing* (William C. Brown Co., 1984), she suggests that kindergarten and elementary children may compare praying to a milk stool. Perhaps someone in your class has seen a milk stool or knows what one looks like. Explain that a milk stool has three legs, and all three legs must be the same length in order to keep your balance on the stool.

Like the stool, we have three types of prayer, and they are all important for us to keep our balance. The first leg is private prayer or praying to God within yourself. This kind of praying can be done anytime and anywhere. You only need God and yourself. The second leg is prayer in a small group that you know, like your family or your class. The group is usually very special to you. The third leg is praying in church or a large group, some of the people you know and some of the people you may not know. Often these prayers are familiar, because they are prayers that we know and use often. Sometimes we call these liturgical prayers. At other times, we pray in a large group, and one person leads the prayer and uses his or her own words. But in these prayers you know that you are a part of the bigger family of God.

The following exercise is one I have adapted from two sources: Marlene Halpin's book,

Puddles of Knowing, and *God Is With Us*, a media kit developed by Cecile Beam and published by Graded Press. The exercise will guide your students in personal or quiet prayer. You may substitute colors, trees, birds, flowers, or other things for the water. No particular body position is necessary, but they will need to be comfortable. Read the suggestions slowly and quietly, pausing to let the students imagine.

First, I want you to find your own place in the room. You may want to sit or to lie down. It may be near someone else or in a corner by yourself, but you must have room to stretch your hands out without touching another person.

What is your private space like? I think I'll paint mine blue. Do you want to paint yours? (pretend to paint) You can build a wall on all sides to make your place more private if you want. (pretend to build) Make a window in the wall if you like. Do you have cushions in your place? (fluff up pillows) Is it dark or bright?

Now, I want you to close your eyes and imagine that you are a drop of water. Sometimes there may be other drops of water around you, and sometimes you may be alone. There is a rainbow overhead.

Where are you? Imagine the place where you are. Are you in a river, moving slowly toward the ocean? Are you in a creek, laughing as you skip over rocks? Are you in a lake, or an ocean? What is going on around you? Are there fish? Is an animal coming to drink? Are children playing? Are you turning a water wheel?

Now you change from running water to another type of water. How do you change? You decide how you will change and see it inside yourself. What's happening to the other drops around you? What about the rainbow? What does it do?

(After a long pause) Now, let the imagining fade away. Come back to our classroom and be yourself, but remember how you felt.

(Give time for an adjustment to the change.) Would anyone like to tell us how you felt? You don't have to if you don't want to, because that was in your private place, but I would enjoy hearing about how some of you felt.

As the students tell of their feelings, ask them about what was happening in their imaginations as they had those feelings. Listen to each one and recognize each feeling as an o.k. feeling. Ask them occasionally where the rainbow was when they were having that feeling. If they don't know, you might suggest that they close their eyes again and go back into their imagining and let that part come. Take time for this.

After such a quiet exercise, tell them that you are going to take some time for each of them to get to know the really-really me inside themselves. Ask them to close their eyes again and relax. Ask them to listen to their own breathing, in and out, as you say, "Breath in; breath out." Do this slowly at first, then faster, then slowly again. Then suggest the following:

Think about yourself. Where is the really-really me part of yourself? Is the really-really you your arm? Is it your foot? Is it your head? What part of you laughs and cries? What part of you loves, and what part feels great when you do something for someone else? That part is the really-really you.

Now, take the really-really you part of you deep inside yourself. Take it into your heart. Invite God to come into your heart. Invite God to come into your heart with the really-really you. Show God the special things about yourself. Show God how you felt as you imagined you were a drop of water. Show God what the rainbow did in your imagination. Show God anything else that you want to about yourself or about what's happened this week.

Bring people who are special into your heart, too. Show them to God. Show God anything special about them. Is it a special time? Is one of them having trouble? Is there something that you've talked to this special person about or something that you want to talk with him or her about? Tell God about how you love these special persons and about how they love you. Now let the really-really you and God love them together.

Let the thoughts of those people fade out of your mind, but continue to love them. Right now just God and the really-really you are in your heart. Let God love you. Think about how that love feels, all around you. Enjoy just being with God. Enjoy the love. Listen to what God may have to say to you.

(After a pause) Open your eyes slowly. (Another pause) Let's say together the prayer that Jesus taught us, "Our Father . . . ."

Sometimes you will want to use only the last part of this experience beginning with "Right now just God and the really-really you are in your heart." Close that paragraph by asking them to listen to what God may have to say to them about some specific thoughts taken from the curriculum of the day or something that is of concern in your church or community. Some classes may respond to using this as a routine closing for your class.

With young children, you will want to use selected parts of the experience. Remember that their attention span is much shorter and tailor the time accordingly.

Older children and youth can identify the parts of prayer that are used in this experience. The thoughts about the rainbow may have spurred a prayer of adoration. Some of the students may have used the time to show God something about themselves or about their week as a prayer of thanksgiving or confession. When they brought people who were special into their hearts, they were praying prayers of intercession. Their time of listening to God may be a form of supplication.

After the students have had such experiences in quiet prayer, try to provide a quiet place in the room where individuals may go anytime they want. There are many ways that you can set up this place, but it is important that it be uncluttered. Change it frequently instead of putting all of your ideas into it at one time.

The quiet place may be created by moving furniture, draping material, or just piling fluffy pillows in a corner. Help the students feel free to use the quiet place from time to time. You may add a few books that show God's world or a record player and earphones for some instrumental music.

A large basket of shells is good for such a place to encourage thinking about how the animal that lived in the shell must have felt on the ocean floor, or look at all the colors in the shell. They may want to feel the shell to find its smooth parts and rough parts. Just holding the shell and wondering about it can lead to meditation and prayer.

Poem Prayers

Very few of us have the talents of true poets, but we can all express ourselves in some sort of free verse. Experiment with various styles yourself, and select several to try at different times. Some students will enjoy one type more than another. After you have worked with several, allow the students to choose their own style.

You may want to suggest the subject for the prayer poems. Perhaps it will be something that relates to your curriculum. It may be thanking God for something that you have seen in God's world or for people who are special to them. It may be thanking God for Jesus or for some truth that you have learned in the Bible. It may be asking God to be with the student in a particular situation.

Some examples of a variety of types of poems follows. Since this type of prayer requires reading and writing skills, the activities are most appropriate for older children and youth. However, teachers of younger children may adapt the activity by making it a class activity, drawing ideas from the class and the teacher doing the writing on a chalkboard.

1. **Picture poems** are words or phrases that are written in the outline shape of an object. If the prayer is for God's world, the student may select to write the poem in the shape of a tree or a flower. If the prayer is about how we change, you may suggest that the poem prayer be written in the shape of a butterfly. A Lenten prayer may be written in the form of a cross. Allow the students to decide on their own shapes as they become familiar with the method.

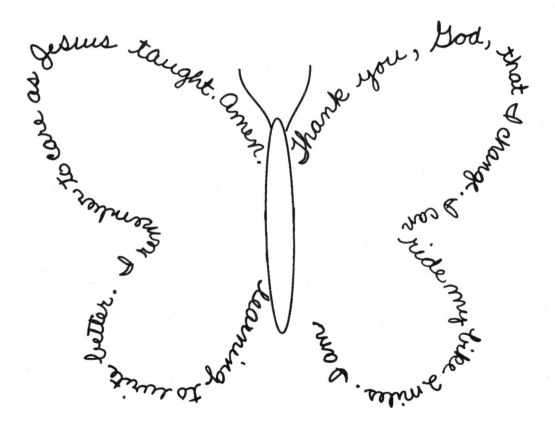

2. The **cinquain** (sin cane) poetic form has five lines. It is very effective for a prayer of thanks, or it may be a praise prayer. Older children may use it as a request for help with a special problem.
Line 1: One word title or subject.
Line 2: Two words that tell about the subject. They may be a phrase or separate words.
Line 3: Three action words (verbs or "ing" words) or a phrase about the subject.
Line 4: Four words that tell of a feeling about the subject.
Line 5: The subject word again or another word that means the same. Or you may wish to use Amen here.

Here are two examples:

Trees

Leaves, branches

Swaying, rustling, reaching

A gift from God.

Shade

* * * * * * * *

Namecalling

Unfriendly, unloving

Hurting, painful, distressing

I forgive and love.

Amen

3. **Free verse** can take various forms. The lines may be any length. They may be phrases, sentences, or a series of words. With young children, suggest that they give you two short lines about something they are thankful for. Title it with the subject and add an Amen or Thanks at the end.

4. Children enjoy **repetition**. Try creating a poem prayer by beginning each line of the poem with the same word.
   Friends laugh with me when I'm happy.
   Friends cry with me when I'm sad.
   Friends love me even when I'm angry.
   Friends are friends, no matter what.
   Thank you, God, for friends.
Another form of a repetition prayer repeats a short sentence every other line. The sentence may be about the subject, or it may be a response of praise or thanks.

I saw the pink sunrise this morning.
Thank you, God, for the colors.
A red bird flew by my window.
Thank you, God, for the colors.
I found yellow dandelions on the lawn.
Thank you, God, for the colors.
The bright blue sky became dark at night.
Thank you, God, for the colors.
Amen.

5. Try a **pop-up prayer** poem. This is one that has a few short sentences or phrases and just seems to pop into your mind. It can come after you have spent some time thinking about a subject or just relaxing with God inside yourself. One of my pop-up prayers is:

Oh God,
Fall is a time the world seems to die.
But we come alive with
new schedules
new shirt sizes
new plans.
Perhaps it's because we know
you are a dependable God.
We know you send
new life each spring.
Amen.

6. A prayer poem of the **senses** is one to which children can relate. This poem thanks God for a subject and tells about that subject, using the five senses.

Thank you, God, for my friend.
I see her, and I am happy.
I hear her voice; it sounds glad.
I taste the lunch we share.
I smell the flowers as we walk together.
I feel important when I am with her.
Thank you, God.

You can also make a prayer poem using only one of the senses. It might be a prayer thanking God for food and describing how each food tastes. Or it might be a prayer thanking God for one of the senses.

I hear the birds sing early in the morning.
I hear the voices of my friends at school.
I hear the noise of traffic.
I heart the water as it fills the bath tub.
I hear my mother (father) tell me "I love you."
Thank you, God, for ears to hear.

Prayer Notebooks

You may make prayer notebooks with any age student. With young children, make a small booklet with pictures that tell about the prayer. Very young children may find pictures of favorite foods or of animals in magazines. If the child is too young to cut and paste, do this for them as they watch. Let them decide where they want to place the pictures in the book and arrange them on the page. They can help you push the picture into place and press it to make the paste stick. After you have pasted the pictures in the book, pray the prayer together, saying "Thank you God for . . . " Have the child point to each picture so that he/she decides what you will thank God for together. Older children may draw the pictures.

Encourage children who can write to have a prayer notebook that they add to from time to time. This is a good foundation for journaling. You may even want this to be a part of a quiet time at the end of each class session. Stress the fact that the prayers do not need to be in the usual prayer form but may be in any form, even a letter to God.

Make a special box or select a special drawer where the notebooks will be stored. Assure the students that it is their own private prayer journal and that you will not read it. If they have something that they want you to read at any time, they can bring it to you, but what they write in it is between them and God.

Each student may want to draw a design on the cover or decorate it in some way. Consider making a prayer crest for the cover. Information on a prayer crest is given at the end of this chapter.

Youth may elect to put their prayers in a three-ring binder so they can add their own prayers to the book as well as other prayers they discover that are helpful to them.

Some of these may be prayers to memorize which can be quickly and easily called forth to give comfort and express joy.

Prayer Puzzles

There are several creative ways that you may help children form their own prayers by giving them starters in puzzle form and they add their own words. Puzzles give the framework for a prayer that students can build on. Here are a few to try, or you may create your own.

1. Word puzzle
    Use the letters in a word as the beginning letters of words, phrases, or sentences in a prayer:

    E very person
    A pples
    R ivers
    T rees
    H ome I give you thanks, O God.

2. Bouncing Ball Prayer Puzzle

Fill in words in this prayer to make your own prayer:

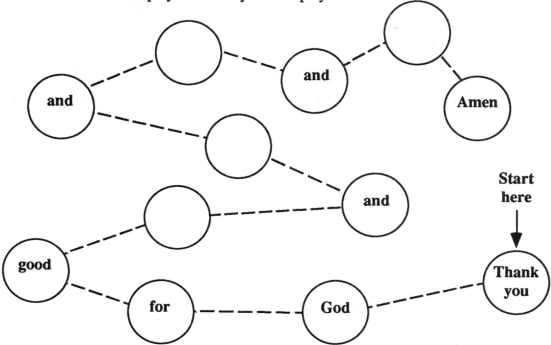

3. Pyramid Prayer Puzzle

Look at the sample below. This prayer begins with one idea written on the large building block. One to three more blocks were added with nouns of that category written on each block. As the student thinks of words that are related to each of these nouns, additional blocks and words are added.

The first time this type of puzzle is introduced to the class, do it together on the chalkboard and use just one or two categories until they get the idea of how to do it. You might provide a printed form with blank blocks, and just the word idea and categories you wish to use for the prayer filled in. When the class is proficient, they can create their own pyramids form scratch.

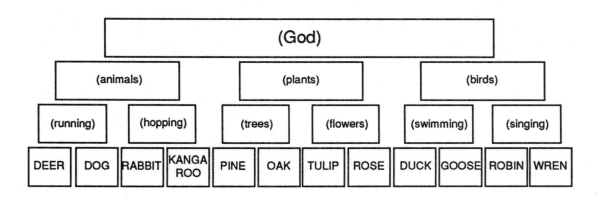

4. Overturned Prayer

Taking 3 by 5 cards, the students list something that they enjoy, one on each card. This may be such things as food that Mother cooks, playing with my friends, going to Sunday school, taking swimming lessons, and so forth.

They will then write the first part of the prayer of thanks, using these ideas, and turn the card over to write what life would be like for someone who did not have them. For example:

Front side of card   Back side of card

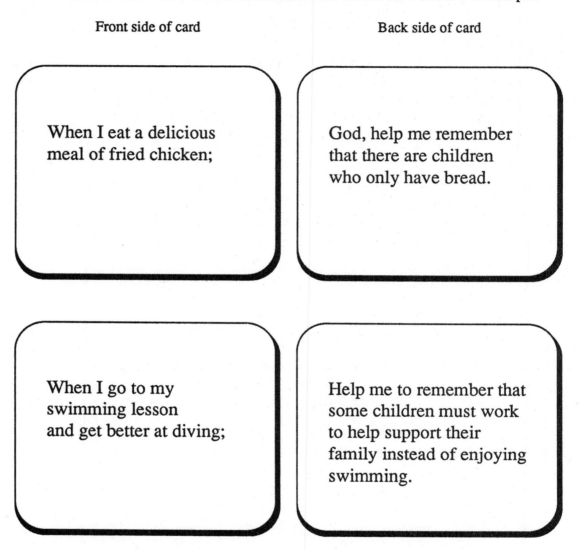

When I eat a delicious
meal of fried chicken;

God, help me remember
that there are children
who only have bread.

When I go to my
swimming lesson
and get better at diving;

Help me to remember that
some children must work
to help support their
family instead of enjoying
swimming.

5. Prayer Path Puzzle

Draw a path or road across a piece of paper. Add stepping stones. Provide the first few words of the prayer, putting one word per stepping stone. Duplicate the page and give to students to finish the prayer and decorate the page. When the children become familiar with this form they can create their own Prayer Path Puzzle from scratch.

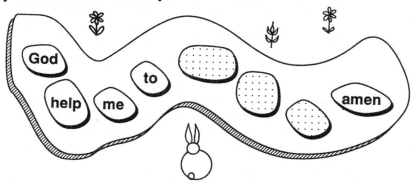

6. Personal Prayer Crest

The crest has been used for many years to tell about a family or a community. It was particularly popular in Europe. Give the following directions: Using the crest shape, make a reminder of particular things that you want to thank God for or that you want to talk with God about in your personal prayers. Write one subject in each space. Each time you pray, use the crest and talk with God about one or more of the subjects on your crest. Make new crests from time to time.

Something about myself I want to change	Someone I want to talk to God about
A time God helped me	A talent I have that I want to thank God for

CHAPTER 6

CREATING GROUP PRAYERS

It is important for children and youth to experience a common bond between themselves and other members of their church school class. One of the foundations of a strong faith development is a relational experience with other Christians.

I have told many church school teachers that if they do nothing else during the year but create a caring community among their students, they have accomplished much. God made us to be relational people. God made us with a need to respond to each other and to our creator.

Group prayers are one of the best ways to establish this relational experience between your students. Group praying may be done using pre-written prayers, such as those suggested in the chapter on memorized prayer. However, when group prayers come out of the experiences of members of the class, there is a closer bonding of Christian love.

Conversational Prayer

Conversational prayer stems from conversation among the group members and listening to God's personal response. We adults participate in this sort of prayer often with a prayer circle. We will ask if there are any special concerns that members want to lift up in prayer before the prayer time begins. Then we will move around the circle, each person praying a few sentences, often about specifics that were suggested by the group members. Usually, the leader sums up the prayer at the close of the meeting, praying for any concerns not mentioned by others.

This style of prayer can be threatening if the students feel pressed to pray in turn. It is also a more formal prayer that some may feel they must endure. I'd like to suggest a more informal style of conversational prayer.

One of the best ways to initiate conversational prayer into your class is to spend some time talking together about the type of week that the students had. Do not call this prayer, just conversation. Guide the conversation by using a bean bag made with one design on one side and another design on the other side. One side will represent good things that happened this week, and the other will represent not-so-good things. (I prefer to use the term not-so-good , because this gives a broader range of experiences to choose from. What may seem "bad" to one person may not appear to be "bad" to another.)

As the children move into an age where they can grasp the concept of cause and effect, they may see some of the good that comes from the not-so-good. This is the realization that we get from Romans 8:28, "We know that in all things God works for good with those who love him, those whom he has called according to his purpose."

It is important that the class sit in a circle for this prayer. This gives a better opportunity for open conversation. Allow the class to decide which side of the beanbag will be used to talk about the good things of the week and which will be used for the not-so-good things. Explain that in your conversation everyone who would like to share will have the opportunity, but that in order for everyone to hear, only the person with the bean bag will talk.

Begin the conversation by placing the bean bag on the floor in front of you with the appropriate side up and sharing an experience you had during the week. Throw the bean bag to someone else who would like to share. They will in turn place the bag on the floor with the appropriate side up as they tell about their experience.

Adults can appreciate such a conversation as a part of the prayer, because we realize that God is with us always and knows all about our week anyway. But if, at first, we present the idea that this is part of our prayer, the students sometimes become inhibited. After you have practiced this for some time and the class feels comfortable about sharing, you might say casually, "When we talk like this together, I'm sure that God is hearing us even before we say that we will pray. Perhaps this is a way of praying, too."

After persons have had the opportunity to tell of their experiences, ask for the bean bag and place it in the center of the circle. Then close the time together with a simple prayer, "God, we come to you with many things that have happened this week, some of them good and some of them not-so-good. We thank you for being with us in all of these times. Amen."

As you work with conversational prayer, you may find it appropriate to pause occasionally between sharing, if there is something that has been particularly stressful for a student. Let there be a prayer for quiet and peace as you lift the occasion up to God. Allow the students to listen to God within themselves instead of filling the space with words.

A Prayer Web

Creating a prayer web with yarn or string can help a class recognize the way that they relate to one another. This prayer gives students an opportunity to contribute to a group prayer which will then be closed with an inclusive sentence, asking God to hear all that we have said. A prayer web is most appropriate for prayers of thanks. Or you may use another theme that is a part of your curriculum.

The class should be in a circle for this prayer. If your room is comfortable, sit on the floor. As you begin, hold on to the end of the string and mention something that you would like to thank God for or to pray about. Then ask if there is someone else who has something to add. Roll the string ball (or older students may throw the ball) to that person, making a string connection between you and that person. After sharing, that person will hold on to the string and roll/throw the ball to another. As you proceed across the circle, you will create a web with the string. If you are rolling the ball, everyone will need to hold the string high during the rolling; if throwing the ball, hold the string next to the floor.

After all who want to speak have shared, include those students who did not share by passing the ball to them so they can take hold of the string and every member of the class is connected to the web. Close the experience with a simple sentence, "God, we ask you to hear all that we have talked about along our prayer web. Amen."

Pre-prayer Discussion

In order to create written group prayers, it is important to precede it with discussion. This discussion may come from a suggestion or a subject in your curriculum, or you may initiate the subject yourself. You may even provide research information for the students to use and report to the group. One such subject might be hunger. There are sources available in public libraries for hunger facts, or you may write to SEEDS, 222 East Lake Drive, Decatur, Georgia 30030 for information. If you are studying baptism, provide materials on different uses for water, and ask the students to research the uses before your discussion.

Summarize your discussion, using the popcorn method. You will need a chalkboard or large sheet of paper for this. Ask the students to pop ideas about your subject to you in the form of words or short phrases. Randomly write these on the board or paper. Using these words or ideas, you will then write a group prayer.

One group did research in the early chapters of Acts to find the characteristics of the early church. They decided that the church was (1) devoted to learning, (2) worshiped together, (3) enjoyed fellowship, (4) shared among themselves and with others. The class then wrote a prayer, asking God to help their class to develop those characteristics.

Litany Prayer

A litany is a form of prayer, most often used in a group. In the litany, one or two lines are followed by a responsive phrase repeated by the entire group. This phrase is usually repetitive, although youth and children who read easily may enjoy some variation in the wording.

Children particularly enjoy litany prayers because they provide opportunity for verbal participation without the embarrassment of not knowing what to pray. When the litany is written by the children, they know the words before they offer the prayer. This takes away any pressure of thinking about what to say.

The litany grows out of personal feelings and concerns when it is written as part of the class experience. Printed litanies or litanies prepared by one person may not reflect the personal feelings of the group.

Use the central theme for the litany as the title. Help the students plan a theme and title that relates to their study.

As ideas on the theme of the litany are offered, write them on a large piece of paper or on a chalkboard. Then agree on a response. You may use scripture passages or a phrase from a song as the response. Write this on a separate paper. Organize the ideas into some sort of pattern. Cut the statements apart and arrange them in order.

You may want to write a sentence of introduction for the worship leader, although it is not necessary. Use the litany for the worship experience. Tape strips with the statements together for reading, with the understanding that there is a response between each statement.

Use the names or initials of each student beside his or her contribution. When the litany is used in worship, ask each to read his or her own contribution.

The litany is not a performance, even when used before other people. Use simple language, even conversational tone. We want students to look on prayer as conversation with God.

The following example uses the theme of "Ways God Talks to Us." The leader, individuals, or small groups may read the sentences in regular print, and the total group reads the responses printed in boldface type.

Ways God Talks to Us Today

Leader: Jesus spoke to Paul on the road to Damascus, and God also speaks to us today. God speaks through the Bible.
We Listen, God, As You Talk.
Leader: Teachers and preachers tell us of God.
We Listen, God, As You Talk.
Leader: God talks to us through parents and friends.
We Listen, God, As You Talk.
Leader: We can hear God speak in the wind and in the quiet of the early morning.
We Listen, God, As You Talk.
Leader: God is within me and talks to my inner self.
Help Me, God, To Listen For You Every Day And At All Times. Amen. [1]

Echo Pantomime

Echo pantomime has become popular in recent years among teachers of children. I have also used it effectively with youth and adults. You can create your own echo pantomime. Divide the prayer into short phrases or sentences. (Young children will need to have the prayer broken frequently.) Consider a simple movement for each phrase or sentence. Practice the echo pantomime before the session so that you have it well in mind and feel comfortable with it. Some teachers find it helpful to write the pantomime on a large paper and post it high on the wall behind the students so that the teacher can see it while facing the students. Older children and youth can create their own echo pantomime prayer.

Before using an echo pantomime, talk with the children about what an echo is. Tell them that to pantomime is to act something out. Explain that you will say a few words of the prayer with some actions, and they will repeat the words, using the same actions. Here is an example of an echo pantomime appropriate for younger children.

Example:

Prayer	Action
Dear God, we thank you: For the sunshine	Make large sun with both arms.
For the rain	Moving fingers, lower hands.
For the trees that sway in the wind	Sway as a tree.
For the grass and the flowers	Put fingers together and move hands up, as if sprout coming through ground.
Sometimes we're happy;	Smile big and "draw" smile at corners of mouth with fingers.
Sometimes we're sad;	Frown and "draw" frown at corners of mouth with fingers.
But we know that you love us.	Fold arms across chest in "hug".
Amen.	Hands up, looking up.

Movement Prayers

When we incorporate movement into our prayers, we are loving God with our whole selves, with our body as well as our heart and mind. Movement may be a part of the prayers that the class creates or it may be adapted to printed prayers. Young children can participate in very concrete movements. Older children and youth can understand movement that symbolizes a feeling or an attitude. Some of our prayers from the early church heritage are more meaningful to children when we add movement to them. Prayer hymns are easily adapted to movement prayers.

Young children can enjoy making movements similar to an animal as they thank God for the animal. Or they may "sprout" from the ground as a blade of grass or open their arms to the sunshine as a flower. They can curl up in a ball, as if inside a seed, then let their hands form the sprout when the sun warms the ground. Encourage them to create their own movements. These can be simple thank you prayers to God.

Older children and youth can experiment with movements ahead of time, then plan for a series of movements to use with the prayers. It is important that the students create and plan the movement as expressions of their feelings as the words of the prayer are said or sung. The teacher can be helpful by making suggestions of movements and helping the students experiment until they find the movement they want. Talk about the prayer and the meanings of the words. Ask them how they might express the meaning of a particular word or phrase without using words. Give them opportunity to experiment and decide what movements they want to use.

As you decide which movements to use for particular parts of the prayer, remember that every word or phrase does not have to have a movement. This would make the prayer too cluttered with action to appreciate the mood.

Be sure that the movements are simple. The movement prayer is not a performance, but rather a communication between the participant and God. Never "practice" the prayer, but pray it. If one person expresses him/herself differently from another, welcome this as the student's own communication with God. Everyone does not have to do exactly the same thing.

Here are some possible movements that may come out of your group:

Approaching God	Step forward, head held high
Praise	Uplifted head and upward movement of arms
Receiving gifts; Holy Spirit	Head bowed, arms curved over head with fingertips touching
Communicating	Hand movement from lips upward as if to God and outward as if to others
Heaven and earth	One arm stretched up and in front; other arm stretched down and behind
Whole universe	With right hand, circle left to right
Springtime; new birth	Hands together at chest and then moving upward, as sprouts coming from earth
Fellowship	Arms across neighbors' shoulder
Unity	Clasping neighbors' hands
Rejecting evil	Hands to sides, lowered and pushing back
Repentance	Kneeling, looking above and then bowing head
Amen	Head bowed, arms relaxed

Scripture Paraphrased Prayer

Paraphrasing is a good way to understand scripture. Older children and youth will be able to look up passages and work with paraphrasing by themselves. With younger children, read the verse together and talk about how you could say the same thing in different words. The paraphrased scripture can then be used in a prayer. You may want to create a litany prayer with it.

Here is an example of verses that students may paraphrase and sample responses:

God Brings Growth

God made everything and was happy with it. (Genesis 1:31)
Thank you, God, for your plan for growth.
God has a time for everything. (Ecclesiastes 3:1)

Thank you, God, that we grow from babies to adults.
To be a friend, we always love. (Proverbs 17:17a)
Help us, God, to remember our friends.
Be loving to each other. Forgive each other as Christ taught. (Ephesians 4:32)
We will try to use our actions to produce good feelings, dear God.
It is good to grow up in all ways. (Ephesians 4:15)
Our minds continue to grow no matter what our age. Thank you, God.
We are shown God in many ways. (Deuteronomy 4:35b)
We thank you, God, that we understand more about you each day.
Thank you, God, for growth.
Amen.

Table of Thanks

Set aside a table that will be your praise table or table of thanks. The students may make a large sign, illustrating it with gifts from God.

On the table, place a few objects that remind us of gifts for which we can thank God. The gifts may be food gifts, gifts from nature, gifts of relationships, or gifts of love from other people. Suggest that students look for symbols of gifts during the week and bring them to place on the table.

Sometime during the session, plan to spend time at the table talking together about God's gifts that are displayed on the table. Offer thanks in prayer, asking the students to mention something from the table between responses such as "Thank you, God, for your gift of _____."

Flat Pictures Prayer

Assemble a number of pictures on a particular subject. These may be magazine pictures or pictures from your church school picture file. Spread the pictures out on the floor and ask each student to select one picture that reminds them of something they would like to talk to God about in your group prayer.

For younger children, you might make this a thanksgiving prayer. The pictures may show food, clothing, animals, parents, etc. Use statements and questions such as these to help the students:

• Select a picture that shows something you like very much. You can pretend that the pictures of people are special people that you like.

• I would like for you to tell us something about your picture. (Allow the students to tell as they are ready, but do not insist on any one talking who doesn't want to.)

• These are special things and people that God has given us. Let's thank God for them. "Thank you, God, for all that you have given us. Amen."

Elementary age children and youth might develop an intercessory prayer for persons in other countries and consider our responsibility to take Christ to all the world. Use pictures of persons from other countries. Adapt the following statements and questions to the pictures you have available:

- Select a picture from those laid out.
- In what ways does that person look like you?
- How is he or she different?
- Look at where the person is. How is it alike or different from where you live?
- Do you suppose your person speaks English?
- If not, how do you think he or she feels when they hear English?
- Does your person look as if he or she is happy or sad? What do you suppose made him or her happy or sad?
- If you could talk with the person, what would you say?
- What favorite Bible story might you tell him or her?
- Let's pray a prayer of intercession, remembering the people of other countries, trusting them to God and asking God to show us how we can help them. "Our God, we cannot go to other countries now to personally share the stories of Jesus with these people. But we want them to feel very near to you. We know that they have some problems like ours and some that are different from ours. We know that you can help them, and we will help by sending others to share with them. Amen."

Older children and youth can use pictures to stimulate and focus meditation. Pictures of people in life situations are good for this. Here is an example of questions and statements you might use to guide them:

- From the selection of pictures, choose one.
- What do you think happened just before this picture was frozen for you to see?
- Look at one person in the picture. Give the person a name.
- How do you think your person is feeling?
- What do you think your person's needs are?
- Say a prayer for your person.
- What are some things that could have happened in the next few minutes after the picture?
- Introduce your person to the group. (Each person, as they are ready to do so, holds their picture so all can see it and starts by saying, "This is (Mary). She (he) . . .)

After the meditation, close with a simple prayer asking God to help us all be more sensitive to the needs of those around us.

1. Delia Halverson, *Grades 5-6 Teacher, Vacation Bible School*, 1987 (Graded Press: Nashville), p. 48.

CHAPTER 7

CREATING PRAYERS USING ART

No two people learn the same things from the same experience. If we are to teach prayer then we must be prepared to introduce prayer with a variety of methods. Likewise, no two teachers are comfortable with the same combination of methods. You must consider your students and consider yourself as you select the approach you will take with your class.

Creating original prayers with art is natural with children. As we grow older, we often suppress our creativity and become inhibited. Conversations can foster the student's creativity. Acceptance of a person's work can encourage creativity. Use art as a means of helping the search for God within, then use the art expression as a way for the students to share with you or the group, the thoughts they had as they were creating.

It is important to remember that you are using art as a method of praying, not to achieve some finished product for display. The simple act of creation lays a foundation for a deeper relationship with our Creator-God. I so often have to remind myself, when working with children, "It is in the doing that the growing occurs, not in the finished product." Naturally, we want children to have pride in their art expression, but we need to realize that we are church school teachers and not teaching art. Use art as a tool and allow the students to work with the art at their own pace and in their own way.

When we consider art as a tool, we can keep our teaching environment fresh and active. Very little art needs to be displayed in the classroom more than a few weeks, and much of it is more effective if the children take it home where they live seven days a week. It then acts as a reminder that God is with them each day, that we can pray to God anywhere.

First, experiment with the method yourself. This is particularly important with art. Although each method suggested here will have a list of materials, by experimenting you will be sure that you are prepared. (**NOTE:** Try to avoid the use of food as you work with art. When we use food as non-food items and later try to initiate concern for people who are hungry, we are sending mixed signals. We are saying on one hand that food is important and should not be wasted, and we are saying on the other hand that food is o.k. to waste by gluing it to a picture.)

Art is used in most curriculum as a way of responding to what was learned. Since students are used to the focus turning to their creativity, we will need to work on turning the focus from their creation to the experience and feelings that come about as they use art. As I suggested earlier, there is no requirement that we bow our heads and close our eyes to pray. As the students consider their art and work on it, they are actually praying.

You can make these experiences different from the usual curriculum art project by encouraging them to tell you about the feelings they had as they worked. As you make individual comments during the experience, begin with a positive statement about the piece, but move on to conversation about the feelings that the student is having or what the student is thinking during the process. Remember, in this use of art more than any other, the experience is in the doing, not the finished product.

As you display the art in the classroom, talk about how it reminds us of "what we thank God for" or of "how we want to ask God to help us." This focuses on the experience instead of the finished project. When the art goes home, suggest that they use their art to remember the prayer and pray it at home. Encourage them to pray the prayer with their family. If it is a personal prayer, suggest that they place it in their room where they can see it and pray the prayer before they get out of bed in the morning or at night before they go to sleep.

Picture Prayers

Drawing or painting pictures is such a common art project that we often think of it *as* art. Because it requires so little preparation time on the part of the teacher, it is often over-used or used with little student preparation. Since each person learns differently, be sure that you use a variety of art methods with prayer and do not over-use art as a teaching method.

Recognize that creating a picture is placing a part of yourself on the paper. This part of self is very important. It is a part of the student's individualism and self esteem. When talking with a child about the picture, begin with a positive expression such as: "You have used such lovely colors in the picture. Will you tell me about it?" What they see clearly in their drawings we may mistakenly take as something else. Therefore, it is important to encourage a child's interpretation first. Then you will want to encourage the child to talk about feelings or thoughts that he or she had during the creating process.

Use research or conversation as a preparation for drawing. If you are working with a prayer of thanks, talk about God's creation or about friends and helpers for which we are thankful. Picture prayers can also be used as you pray about relationships between people. These may include pictures of friends playing together happily, or older children or youth may draw a picture of a problem in a relationship that he or she wishes to talk with God about.

The drawing experience itself becomes the prayer. As the student draws, the mind and the heart are active in the process. The praying takes place within.

Materials needed:
- Paper (size depending on use)
- Crayons, markers, chalk, or tempera paints and brushes

Finger Painting

Finger painting adds the dimension of movement to the experience of painting, and this can help to make the prayer internal. It is an ideal method to use during a guided meditation. If you do not guide the students' thoughts during the prayer but only offer suggestions for thoughts before hand, you may want to play music as they pray.

If your class has never used finger paints before, allow time for experimentation before you begin to talk about the prayer. First use of finger paints always brings strange comments from the students, and it is better that these comments be aired ahead of time so that they can then focus on the thoughts of the prayer.

Most children enjoy finger painting, but some parents have made such a strong issue over the importance of "keeping clean" that the child cannot experience the joy of finger painting for fear he or she will meet disapproval from the parent. Use your own judgment in such cases. Don't push any art experience onto a child. If they refuse, suggest that they sit and watch the others and think the prayer through in their own minds, or supply another form of art for the child. We often think fingerpaint is just for very young children, but it can be effectively used with older children and youth. Finger paint, music, and a suggested topic can produce a very meaningful experience for older children, youth and even adults.

Finger painting requires a thicker paint than your usual painting. There are commercial finger paints on the market, or you can make your own by adding a little dry tempera to liquid starch. Some preschools have used puddings as finger paints; however, this sends mixed signals about the importance of food as suggested at the beginning of this chapter.

Materials needed:
- Finger paint
- Finger paint paper or shelf (shiny) paper (or a smooth surface such as cookie sheets or trays)
- Old shirts or smocks to protect clothing

Prepare the paper or surface by dampening it with a sponge. If you are using paper, wetting the surface also helps the paper stay in place. Place the shiny side of the paper up. Place a few tablespoons of the paint on the paper or surface. The children will move the paint around with their fingers to make pictures, designs, or impressions. They can also use their fist, palm, or even forearm. (Be sure sleeves are pushed up out of the way.)

Stained Glass Prayers

Stained glass windows were first placed in churches when the common people could not read and did not have the printed Bible available. They were reminders, or symbols, of Bible stories and of biblical concepts. By looking at the windows, the people could recall the stories themselves.

Creating an object that looks like a piece of stained glass is an exciting way of praying. Symbols lend themselves well to this medium, and the stained glass can be used as a reminder in later prayers.

Materials needed:
- White paper (typing weight)
- Black construction paper
- Pencils, crayons, and scissors
- Black permanent marker
- Cooking oil
- Cotton swabs
- Table protection and paper towels

Pre-cut frames from black construction paper, cutting out the space where the picture will show through.

After conversation about the subject of your prayer, discuss possible ways to illustrate the prayer. Place the pre-cut black construction paper frame over the paper and draw an outline of the opening. (After the picture is finished, the "opening" area will be treated with oil, but the area outside the "opening" will be left white and not treated with oil.)

Inside the open area, draw the symbol or picture outline with pencil and trace over it with black permanent marker. This will represent the "leaded" part of the stained glass. Using crayons, color all parts inside the opening area, including the background.

Protect the working surface with papers. Using cotton swabs dipped in cooking oil, coat the back side of the paper, being careful not to use the oil outside the colored area. Wipe any excess with paper towels.

Glue the frame around the picture.

(**NOTE:** To adapt this for young children, you may want to make several patterns of symbols that a child may select from, such as foods that we are thankful for. You will have to help the child trace the pattern and fill in the permanent markings.)

59

Poster or Banner prayers

Posters or banners are more permanent reminders of prayer. You may want to use this medium to share your prayers with the rest of the church.

Materials needed:
- Large pieces of heavy cloth such as felt or heavy rolled paper. Cut to make individual banners 15" x 18" or smaller.
- For cloth banners: medium to small pieces of multi-colored, multi-textured cloth, lace, rick-rack, etc.
- For paper banners: crayons, markers, tempera paint, or colored paper
- Glue (white or fabric glue), needles and thread
- Scissors and pencils
- Large paper for planning sketches, grocery sacks for patterns
- Hanging device such as dowel sticks or broom handles and string or cord (masking tape for paper banners)

Here are several ways to use banners:

1. The banner may be a prayer of adoration. You might talk first about parts of God's world that reminds you of the greatness of God. Each person may make his or her own banner selecting one of these things as the center of the design, or you may incorporate several ideas into a class banner. Or you might make a banner using stylized designs of ways that we praise God. The line drawings in the Good News Bible are an excellent source for this. The banner may be used in future class sessions to focus your minds on a prayer of adoration.

2. Prayers of thanksgiving can come from a banner experience. These naturally follow conversations about things for which we are thankful. They may be people, God's world, experiences, foods, etc.

3. Concern for others can be a center focus of a banner. This becomes an intercessory prayer. It may follow a study of persons in another country or people in need in your own city. The banner may be as simple as hands reaching out to each other or it might display photographs taken around your neighborhood.

Select your theme and jot down words, shapes, and colors that remind you of this idea. Make drawings on paper of how the words and shapes might fit together, deciding on your basic design.

If you are making a cloth banner, make a full size paper pattern for each color. You will also want to make patterns for the letters of any words you plan to use. These are then moved about on the background fabric to get a better idea of how the finished product will look. For paper banners, pencil in the design and color it last.

Pin the patterns on the appropriate colored pieces of fabric and cut them out. Glue or sew them in place. You may wish to attach other decorations such as braid, buttons, etc.

The top of the banner may be finished with a hem large enough to hold the wooden dowel and a string or cord tied to both ends of a dowel. The bottom may be finished by hemming, cutting scallops or points, or attaching a fringe.

The banners may be taken home and used in their prayer times at home, or you may want to use them in future class sessions to focus your prayers. If you have developed a quiet place in your room, include a banner in it, but change it periodically so that fresh prayer thoughts come from the banners. You may also be able to use the banner in the Sanctuary for special worship services.

Prayer Collage

A collage offers a three dimensional expression of prayer, using an assortment of items that may be attached to a surface. It may be done as a class prayer, or each student may prepare individual prayers.

Materials needed:
- For background or surface: construction paper, cardboard or box tops, pieces of wood, paper plates, etc.
- Assortment of items for selecting, such as: various colored or textured paper to be cut or torn into shapes, straws, egg shells, cotton balls, fabrics, lace, fur or leather scraps, small stones, shells, wood shavings, dried grasses and seeds, packing materials, buttons, etc. (Note the reference to use of food at the beginning of this chapter.)
- White or other strong glue

Begin by exploring the variety of materials that you have provided for the collage. Spend some time talking about specific items and what they remind you of or feelings that you have when you see or touch the items.

If you are creating a thank you prayer, you might consider thanking God for textures and create a collage of various textures. Talk about how some things are rough and some are smooth. There are some things that are smooth and rough, such as an ear of corn. God created all sorts of textures.

Another prayer might include persons who are a part of the student's life. The objects might symbolize these persons or ways that the persons care, such as a bit of rick-rack to remember that Mother made a dress, a piece of sponge to recall how a sister or brother helped clean up after an accident, a piece of wood shaving to remember the toy that Grandfather made, or shells to remember the enjoyable time that the family had at the beach. Such a prayer as this may be planned a week in advance so that items may be brought from home to use in the collage. It will still be necessary for you to have supplemental items on hand for new ideas and for visitors and others who do not bring their own.

Once the items have been selected for the collage, experiment with ways to arrange them on the background material. Any preparation of the background material such as sanding or painting will need to be done before the items are attached. Attach the items to the collage using white glue, or use a stronger glue for heavy articles.

Prayer Mosaic

A prayer mosaic may be made after conversation about some particular subject, or you may suggest that the students select their own subject for prayer and make a mosaic that tells about the prayer.

Materials needed:
- Rigid background piece: cardboard, playwood, boards, linoleum, styrofoam, or hard plastic
- Materials to be arranged for design: paper (small pieces of colored tissue, construction paper, wrapping paper, etc.), shells, pebbles, small pieces of cloth, colored egg egg shells (broken or crushed), buttons, nut shells, seeds, bark, etc.
- White glue

Mosaics are pictures or designs made from a collection of similar objects. With a pencil, sketch the design on the background material. The most accessible objects to use to fill in the design are small pieces of colored paper. Grouping the colors, the pieces are glued on the background to form the picture or symbols. Use larger pieces with small children and outline the symbols or pictures rather than fill it in completely.

Prayer Chain

I believe that paper chains must have been favorites with children for as long as we have had paper and glue. We have used them primarily for Christmas decorations, but there is no reason why we cannot combine this favorite creative activity with prayer.

Materials needed:
- Construction paper of various colors, cut into strips about 1 x 6 inches
- Glue or tape

During a discussion on the prayer subject, or during a time of private reflection, the student will write or draw specific items for prayer, one item on each strip of paper. Then the strips are made into a chain by interlocking them and taping or gluing the ends of the strips together with the words and/or drawings on the outside. By using the chain, the student remembers what he or she decided to include in the prayer. Each day the child chooses a different link to help focus his or her prayer.

This method may also be used for a group prayer. Each person would have one strip of paper and write on it one item to be included in the group prayer. Then as you pray the prayer, each student mentions his or her item and the class responds with a sentence such as "We thank you, God" as the student attaches his or her strip to the class chain.

Prayer Mobile

A prayer mobile is a useful experience in prayer that can be taken home and serves as a reminder as the student prays each day. Young children will need assistance in assembling a mobile, but they can take part in the selection of the items to make up the mobile. The older the student, the more capable they are of completing their mobiles themselves.

Materials needed:
- Hangers for the mobile: dowel sticks, cardboard paper rolls, wire, small tree branch, coat hangers, or paper plates
- String or yarn for hanging objects
- Objects to be hung from mobile
- Scissors, glue, etc. depending on your objects

A prayer mobile may have objects or pictures that are symbolic of the subjects for which you will pray, or it may be made up of the words that will be used in the prayer itself. If you are drawing pictures or using symbolic objects, talk about what the objects or pictures tell us about the subject. Young children may search for pictures to cut out that remind them of what they want to pray about, such as food, animals, friends, etc. If you are using words, encourage the child to think of his or her own words.

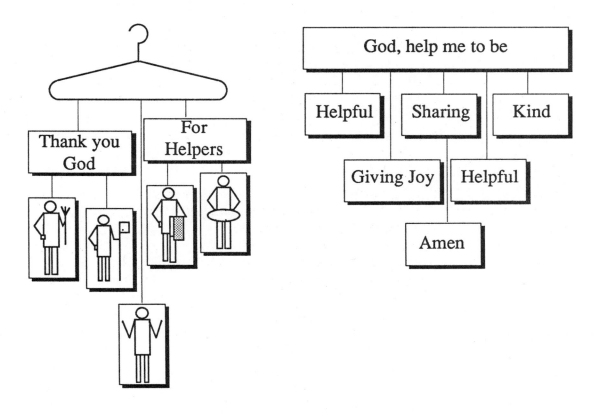

Prayer Pocket

A prayer pocket can contain ideas and thoughts that the student may want to include in his or her prayers. Write thoughts out on paper, to be placed in the pocket.

Materials needed:
- An envelope that has not been used (your choice of size, but consider one small enough to fit inside a Bible)
- Crayons or felt markers for decorating the envelope
- Strips of paper about 1 1/2 by 5 inches

Turn the envelope so that a shorter side is at the top. If the envelope opens along the long side, seal it and cut it open on the short side that is at the top. Decorate the envelope so that it looks like a pocket and put symbols, flowers, and so forth on it.

As you talk about what might be included in a prayer, ideas are written on the strips of paper (or pictures cut out from magazines) and placed in the Prayer Pocket. During a prayer time, give the students opportunity to look through their Prayer Pockets and privately pray for what they have included. Encourage them to place the Prayer Pocket in their Bibles and to use it daily. They can add other prayer thoughts to the Pocket, and if something is no longer appropriate, they can take that out.

Youth may make book covers (paper or fabric) for their Bibles and attach a prayer pocket to the front of the cover.

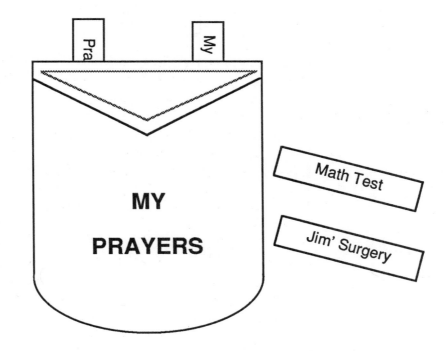

Prayer of Woven Paper

A favorite paper craft with children is weaving strips of paper. This can be used in much the same way that you would use paper chains in prayer, to help us remember what we want to pray about. Elementary age children and youth might recognize paper weaving as symbolic: as Christians, we believe that God uses all things (or weaves together all things) for good. If the strips represent persons for whom you will pray, then the woven prayer may symbolize how we all relate to each other as Christians.

Materials needed:
- Strips of paper of two colors
- Pencils for writing on paper strips

As you consider what is to be included in prayer, the students will write items on the strips. These are then woven together. Place all strips of one color side by side on the table. Taking one strip of the other color, weave over and under those on the table. The first strip may be stapled, taped, or glued in place in order to stabilize the others. The other strips will be left free so that individual strips may be removed and read for prayer and then replaced.

Encourage the students to take the woven mat home and place it under their Bible so that they can use it when they read their Bible and have a personal time with God.

Prayer Cube

The prayer cube is another physical way to remember items that you wish to include in your prayer. You may wish to use general ideas for this instead of specifics. There will be six sides to the prayer cube; each student will decide on six different categories he or she wants to include in prayer. They may include things such as: food, God's world, family members, friends at school, relationships with peers, decisions to be made, ways to help others, our church and church school class, ways the student is growing/changing, and so forth.

Materials needed:
- Square box or poster weight paper or cardboard
- Crayons or felt markers
- Glue or tape if making cube from paper or cardboard

If you can locate a square (or almost square) box, use it. If not, cut out the cube using the drawing below as a guide. The cube should be at least three inches square. If you are making a classroom cube you may want it larger. Wait until the drawings are complete before putting it together.

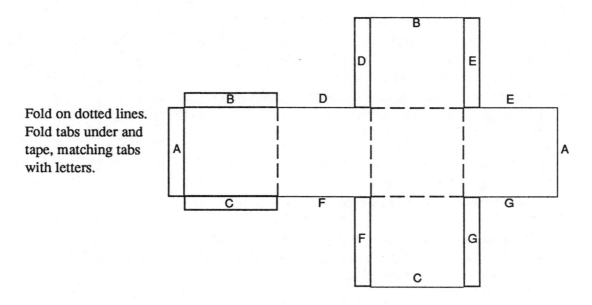

Fold on dotted lines.
Fold tabs under and
tape, matching tabs
with letters.

Each surface on the cube will have a drawing, words, or symbol representing a category for prayer. If you use boxes, make these drawings on separate paper cut to fit on each surface. After the drawings are complete, glue each picture to a surface. If the students construct their own cubes, make the drawings directly on the cube surfaces, then glue or tape the cube together according to the instructions on the above illustration.

One older elementary class made a prayer cube for their classroom. Each side represented something they usually included in their class prayer: an insight that Jesus gave us, something they had learned from the Bible, persons who were sick or lonely, some program of their church, a caring person, a gift from God. During a closing prayer time, a child took the prayer cube and prayed about one category and set it in the middle of the circle. Then another child would pick up the cube and pray about another category and set it down. This would continue until everyone who desired had the opportunity to pray.

If you have someone in your church who is handy with carpentry, you might have a larger cube made from wood. The class can paint symbols or attach pictures to the cube. Such a cube could be reused for other classes by painting a solid color over the original pictures and applying new pictures.

Slide or Filmstrip Prayers

This method can be used when your class creates a group prayer. You may either create a slide prayer by using photo slides that illustrate your prayer, or you may create your own slides or filmstrips using write-on matte acetate material produced for this purpose. If you make your own, be sure that each student makes at least one slide or one frame for the filmstrip.

As you plan your prayer, talk about just what you will want to include. Will it be a prayer that includes several different subjects, or will it be centered around one specific theme? What pictures, words, or symbols might be appropriate for the prayer?

Write the prayer, using some of the methods suggested in chapter 6. Then decide what parts of the prayer you will want to illustrate with the slides or filmstrip.

Materials needed for creating your own slides or filmstrip:
- Old filmstrips and bleach or *35mm Write-On-Film from an audio visual dealer
OR
- Slide mounts (sold commercially) and tracing paper or Write-On-Slides from an audio visual dealer
- Colored ball-point pens, fine tipped permanent markers, or transparency pens and pencils.
- Projector

If you are using an old filmstrip, place it in bleach to remove the color. After it has bleached, rinse thoroughly in clear water. Hang it up to dry, placing a clothes pin or some other heavy object on the bottom of the filmstrip to be sure that it dries without curling. Draw a line across the film at every fourth hole. This will mark off the frames. Draw the illustrations in these frames in order according to your prayer. Allow each drawing to dry before touching so as not to smear the design.

If you are making your slides from scratch, mark off a section on tracing paper just slightly smaller than the size of the slide mounting. Inside this marking, draw the limits of the "window" part of the mounting. Draw and color illustrations for the prayer within the "window" marking on the tracing paper. Cut the picture the size of the outside marking and center the picture so that it shows through the "window" of the slide mounting. Glue or snap the mounting together. Arrange the slides in sequence for the prayer.

If you are using write-on-slides or filmstrip material, draw directly on the matte acetate. Using projection pens and pencils will give you color when projected. These pens and pencils also enable you to "erase" by using a damp tissue.

Photo Prayer Book

A photo prayer book can be planned one Sunday, photos may be taken the next Sunday, and after developing the film the book may be put together on the third Sunday. If you have a longer class period the first two sessions may be combined, and if you use a Polaroid-type camera you may complete it in one session.

Materials needed:
- Camera that is simple to operate and film
- Scrapbook and photo mounting materials

The photo prayer book will be used more as a reminder of specific things to include in personal prayer. However, you will want to have some conversation about just what you will include.

After planning what to include in the book, the students will take photos to be used in the prayer book. You may take a field trip to do this. The photos may be of specific parts of nature, of specific people such as church helpers, of community agencies such as hospitals and nursing homes that care for people, etc. Some students may even want to dramatize specific relational situations to be photographed, such as fighting and forgiving, shunning and friendship, ignoring and helping, etc.

When the photos are developed, the students may write captions to go with each photo in the prayer book. Keep the book available in the classroom for students to pick up and use spontaneously throughout the year. You may want to make several books throughout the year, using themes from your curriculum.

*Available from Ed Tech Service, 17 Commerce St., P.O. Box 407, Chatham, NJ 07928.

CHAPTER 8

MUSICAL PRAYERS

Clap your hands for joy, all peoples!
Praise God with loud songs!

Psalm 47:1

Song has been a part of our religious heritage for thousands of years. It is a natural part of our response to God, and rightly so, for God created music and God created us. God gave us ability to respond to and create music with movement, with instruments, and with our voices.

When our son was a preschooler, he loved to sing. His songs had great enthusiasm but very little tune. He would sing along with us, and I thought, "Poor child, he must be tone deaf because he doesn't stay on key."

Shortly before Sam's sixth birthday, we visited my aunt and uncle. Aunt Elizabeth is much more musical than I am, and she asked him to sit with her at the piano. She would play a note and ask Sam to sing it. When he was not on key, she suggested that he listen to the sound and move his voice up or down until he hit the right note. Sometimes she helped him by playing the note he was singing on the piano, then moving up or down the scale.

Amazingly, Sam had never realized that there was any reason to move his voice around and find the right note. He had just sung random notes for joy! With Aunt Elizabeth's 20-minute start, he went on to sing in All-State Chorus two years in high school and play trombone in All-State Band. He can now listen to a tune and write the notes, as someone else would take shorthand. Music has become a part of his life ministry with youth.

When my father was a child, he was told that he shouldn't sing because he couldn't sing on key. As a pastor, he led many hymns from the pulpit without singing very loudly, until a music director in our church convinced him to sing with the choir in *The Messiah*. For years he had missed this joyful expression of praise and prayer, because someone had squelched his joy for singing in childhood.

Singing Prayers

Some teachers do not know much about music and feel uncomfortable leading it. But it is important that we nurture in our students the joy of expressing themselves through song. Our challenge is not to teach music, but rather to help students praise God and pray in many ways. And singing is an appropriate experience of praise and prayer.

If you do not feel comfortable singing yourself, ask someone else to tape the songs for you and use the tape in your classroom. Use various musical accompaniments where possible, and sometimes use no accompaniment. In a class of youth, you have a good chance of finding someone to play a piano or guitar. Some people sing better with one accompaniment or another. You might want to place only one song on a side of the tape and label it well for quick use.

You might find someone in the church who doesn't want to teach a class regularly but will help you from time to time with music. Just be sure that the person realizes that your goal is not perfect voice blend, but opportunity for expression through singing.

There are many prayer songs that are available in song books, and your curriculum will include them from time to time. Begin a collection of the prayer songs for future reference.

The hymnal is another good source of prayer songs. It is important to help children who take part in congregational worship become familiar with those your congregation uses frequently. Some are prayers of joy and praise, and some are prayers asking God for help or forgiveness. Consider the hymns your congregation uses and read through the words of the hymn, remembering the age of your students. Some words are too abstract for young children, even with explanation. With young children, you may want to use only a few phrases that are appropriate. Choose some appropriate hymns to sing in the classroom. Look over the following list of commonly used hymns to sing as prayers.

Come, Thou Almighty King

Joyful, Joyful, We Adore Thee

Breathe on Me, Breath of God

O Master, Let Me Walk with Thee

Lord, Speak to Me

Open My Eyes, That I May See

Break Thou the Bread of Life (often used in communion)

Holy, Holy, Holy! Lord God Almighty

For the Beauty of the Earth

Have Thine Own Way, Lord

Take My Life, and Let It Be Consecrated

Dear Lord and Father of Mankind

Lord, I Want to Be a Christian

Your hymnal will also have responses and blessings that you sing frequently in your church. Use them in your classroom so that the students can participate in worship with meaning. Some of these may include:

Be Present at Our Table, Lord

Glory Be to the Father (Gloria Patri)

Praise God, from Whom All Blessings Flow (Doxology)

God Be in My Head (Sarum Primer)

Lord, Have Mercy Upon Us (Kyrie Eleison)

The Psalms are a good source of prayer songs. Check the scripture index of your hymnal for songs that are based on psalms. The source of the words of a hymn is printed on the page with the hymn. Some familiar ones are:

O Lord, Our Lord, in All the Earth (Psalm 8)
The Heavens Declare Thy Glory, Lord (Psalm 19)
To Thee, O Lord, Our Hearts We Raise (Psalm 65:13)
O God, Our Help in Ages Past (Psalm 90)
Bless, O My Soul! The Living God (Psalm 103)
Still, Still With Thee (Psalm 139:18)

You can help the students create music to sing with the psalms or with their own prayers. You may want to create a singing response to a prayer litany that the class has written. Here are some suggestions that will help you get started.

1) Taking one phrase of the prayer at a time, say or read the phrase together, feeling the "pulse" and developing a rhythm.
2) Ask various people in the group to speak the phrase individually, using the same rhythm. Talk about how different voices make the phrase sound differently, even when you are using the same words and rhythm. Talk about the "color" sound of each voice, asking what color the voice sounds like. Recognize that God gave us all unique "colors" or sounds in our voices. Affirm the uniqueness of each person's voice.
3) As you go through the phrase again, ask them to listen to the rise and fall of the voice. Tell them that this can be duplicated with music.
4) Ask if someone can think of a tune that might go with the phrase. Allow time to think. You may want to suggest a central tone using whatever instrument you may have on hand. Use the key of C for simplicity, and play the chord C, E, G.
5) Using the student's tune suggestion, sing the phrase together several times.
6) Move on to the next phrases in the same procedure, but repeating the whole song periodically so that you can see how one phrase moves to another.

Another easy way to create a song prayer is to use a familiar tune, even such as "Are You Sleeping, Brother John," and think of words that you may use with that music.
Here are some words for this tune. Your class can write its own words.

Lord we thank you; Lord we thank you,
For our food; for our food.
You have loved us always; you have loved us always;
A-men; A-men.

* * * * * * * *

Lord we thank you; Lord we thank you,
For this day; for this day.
You have made us happy; you have made us happy;
A-men; A-men.

71

Lord we thank you; Lord we thank you,
    For our church; for our church.
    To worship and to serve you; to worship and to serve you
    A-men; A-men.

* * * * * * * *

Lord we thank you; Lord we thank you,
    For your Word; for your Word.
    We can read of Jesus and his friends
        who knew him
    A-men; A-men.

Other Musical Expressions

Singing is not the only way to combine music and prayer. Music can be the backbone of meditative prayer. Recorded instrumental music is best for this, because the child's thoughts are not interrupted by someone else's words. As you hear music that might be appropriate to use as a background for prayer, make a note of it. Where possible, collect tapes that you can have available in the classroom.

Instrumental music is also appropriate for movement prayers. I have a recording that I have used for thirty-five years with children's movement prayers. The record is no longer available, but long ago I copied it on two tapes, one for using and one for saving. It was too valuable a resource to risk being lost.

All children, even if they are hesitant in singing, will respond to accompanying themselves or a recording with musical instruments. These do not need to be purchased instruments. They may be simple instruments that the children make themselves. Consider these suggestions:

Rhythm Sticks

Use 1/2 to 1 inch dowels for the sticks, and cut them in 9 to 12 inch lengths. The children may decorate the sticks with colored markers or paints. A coat of varnish will keep the decoration bright, even with use. The sticks may be used for instruments by hitting them together and hitting them on the floor.

Wrist or Ankle Bells

A set of bells may be made by attaching "jingle bells" to a band of one inch elastic (black elastic is more practical). The bells may be attached by sewing or pinning them on with large safety pins.

Drums

There are various articles that can be used for drums, from an oatmeal box or a large commercial size tin can to a wooden bucket or small keg. Clay flower pots of graduating sizes may be used to produce different tones. Bottles or glasses may be filled with different amounts of water, thereby creating different tones when tapped lightly.

Shakers

Several items may be used in the manner of tambourines. Place small stones, buttons, or acorns between two aluminum pie tins or two hard plastic cups and tape the tins or cups together. These items may also be placed in a box or covered tin can. In some areas of the country, you may find seed pods that rattle when they have dried.

Sandblocks

Select two blocks of wood the same size. They should be easily handled by a child—2 x 4 x 4 inches is appropriate. Cut coarse sandpaper about an inch larger than the blocks and place it on one side of the block, folding the ends over the edge and tacking or stapling them securely. The blocks are rubbed together to make a swishing sound.

CHAPTER 9

AND PRAY FOR YOUR CLASS

And so we've thought of a variety of ways that we can help students to pray creatively in the classroom. Some methods will appeal to some students more than others; some methods will appeal to some teachers more than others. Since prayer is so personal, it is not really measurable. A seed that you plant today may bear its greatest fruit when the child is an adult.

Marlene Halpin, a Dominican sister, developed a prayer room at St. Augustine's School in Kalamazoo, Michigan, where children beginning at age five learned to pray contemplatively. In her book *Puddles of Knowing*, she reflects on the productivity of prayer,

> *Probably nothing is more anti-cultural than prayer. What are we educating for? Productivity. "What do you do?" is a question readily asked of a new acquaintance. In school, work has to be done. At home, work has to be done. At work, work has to be done. In any organization, work has to be done. We need to have something to show what we have done.*
>
> *Not so in prayer. In prayer we are with God. That is enough. We do not produce anything. Nor are we graded. There is no way to compete, be rated, or have a score which is better or worse than another person. There is not even a way to compete with ourselves and surpass our own past performance. That is anti-cultural! We have nothing to show for it—in a tangible, immediate sense.*[1]

What is important, is that we help our students with experiences of prayer, that we put opportunities before them where they can grow in their relationship with God and can pray in a natural way. But we cannot do that effectively if we do not, ourselves, have a prayer relationship with God. You may be able to teach students "book learning" by reading to them from a book, and you may be able to introduce a student to another person when you only know that person slightly.

But prayer is different. Prayer is something that we must experience in order to effectively help others understand it. We must have sat and looked into the face of God if we are to effectively help others find their place in prayer. We cannot share an experience with enthusiasm unless we have been a part of that experience.

Let me suggest that you begin a prayer journal. Purchase a lined notebook that is the size of a Bible, or one of the bound books that are available now with lines for writing. Keep it with your devotional materials, and set aside a special time each day to spend with God. Use the notebook, not in the way you would a diary, but rather as a "conversation" with God. Begin your conversation by inviting God into your heart, then simply "looking and loving." As you wonder over God's greatness, write your thoughts into your prayer journal. Then begin to bring persons and situations into your heart, sharing them with God. The thoughts and feelings that come out of this experience can be written into your prayer journal, too. Be sure to include your students in your prayer. Use the prayer calendar model that is printed at the end of chapter one of this book.

I have used a prayer journal for several years now, sometimes not as regularly as I should. I've never reread most of the pages, and I may never reread them. But just writing the thoughts down helped with my praying process. My prayer journal is not like my other writings where I write, read, and rewrite. I don't have to worry about grammar or spelling. I don't even have to write it so that others can read it! Instead, I write to help process my thoughts. The experience at the time is what counts. Writing the conversations with God helps me to come closer to God. It helps me draw God into my everyday life.

As your prayer life deepens, you will be better able to guide your students into the God/person relationship that we call prayer.

> If I pray eloquent prayers of my church to my children,
>> but do not pray myself,
>>> I am a noisy gong or a clanging symbol.
> And if I lead my children through steps of prayer preparation,
>> but do not take time to talk with God myself,
>>> I am nothing.
> If I place before my children materials for them to use
>> in creating their own prayers,
> But only mouth memorized prayers myself,
>> I gain nothing.
> Prayer is communication with God,
> But I cannot lead others into communication
>> if I only speak lines as if in a drama.
> Prayers of our heritage, prayer patterns, creative activities,
>> these profit me none,
> Unless I spend time with God myself,
>> one on one,
>>> simply lookin' and lovin'.

1. Marlene Halpin, Dominican, *Puddles of Knowing* (Dubuque, Iowa: William C. Brown Company, 1984), p. 47

ADDITIONAL RESOURCES

Beam, Cecile. *God Is With Us* (media kit). Nashville, TN: Graded Press, 1985.

Griggs, Donald L. *Praying and Teaching the Psalms*. Nashville, TN: Abingdon, 1984.

Halpin, Marlene, Dominican. *Puddles of Knowing*. Dubuque, IA: William C. Brown, 1984.

Halverson, Delia T. *Helping Your Child Discover Faith*. Valley Forge, PA: Judson, 1982.

Halverson, Delia T. *Helping Your Child Develop Faith*. Valley Forge, PA: Judson, 1985.

Pockets (a devotional periodical for elementary children). Available from The Upper Room, 1908 Grand Avenue, P.O. Box 189, Nashville, TN 37202.

Psalm Prayers (Five filmstrips and cassette tapes: Interpretations of Psalms 31, 32, 103, 121, and 138), produced by Gerard A. Pottebaum. Treehaus Communications, Inc., P.O. Box 249, Loveland, OH 45140.

Smith, Judy Gattis. *Teaching Children About Prayer*. Brea, CA: Educational Ministries, 1988.

Turner, Rosalie. *My Very Own Book of The Lord's Prayer*. Nashville, TN: Abingdon, 1987.

Webb, Lance. *The Art of Personal Prayer*. Nashville, TN: Abingdon Press, 1962. Now available in paperback from The Upper Room, P.O. Box 189, Nashville TN 37202-0840.

Curriculum:

Practicing Prayer and Praise (Life Box for Junior Highs) Nashville, TN: Graded Press.

Foundations: Basics of the Christian Faith for Youth, Volume 2, "What Does It Mean to Be Spiritual?", Nashville, TN: Graded Press

Teach Us to Pray (grades 2-6), Nashville, TN: Graded Press.

NOTES

NOTES

NOTES